The
HEALTHCARE
CURE

How Sharing Information
Can Make the System Work Better

JEFF MARGOLIS

Founding CEO and Chairman Emeritus of the TriZetto Group, Inc.

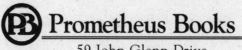

Prometheus Books

59 John Glenn Drive
Amherst, New York 14228–2119

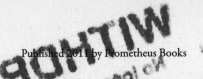

Published 2011 by Prometheus Books

Cover image © 2011, Media Bakery
Cover design by Grace M. Conti-Zilsberger

Inquiries should be addressed to
Prometheus Books
59 John Glenn Drive
Amherst, New York 14228–2119
VOICE: 716–691–0133
FAX: 716–691–0137
WWW.PROMETHEUSBOOKS.COM

15 14 13 12 11   5 4 3 2 1

Library of Congress Cataloging-in-Publication Data

Margolis, Jeff, 1963–
   The healthcare cure : how sharing information can make the system work better / by Jeff Margolis.
       p. cm.
   Includes bibliographical references and index.
   ISBN 978–1–61614–487–6 (pbk.)
   ISBN 978–1–61614–488–3 (ebook)
   I. Title.
   [DNLM: 1. Delivery of Health Care, Integrated. 2. Medical Informatics Applications.
3. Health Resources. 4. Information Dissemination—methods. W 26.55.I4]
       LC—classification not assigned

610.285—dc23
                                                                                    2011028694

Printed in the United States of America

Contents

Foreword

I f you're like most Americans, you were probably born in a hospital or other healthcare setting. Chances are good that you'll eventually die in a hospital or with hospice care. Yet most Americans spend the entire time between birth and death confused about the very healthcare system in which life typically begins and ends.

One common misconception is that "the healthcare system" consists only of your hospital, your doctors' offices, and your pharmacy. However, these are simply small parts of a much larger system, and most of us are unaware of just how many other elements of the system exist and how inextricably linked they are to one another. The interactions, shared information, and incentives among the parts of the system are what make the system run the way it does, warts and all. Understanding how the system works now can help us engineer it to work much more efficiently in the future.

So how can you learn more about this vast and complicated system, and—as part of the system yourself—how can you make it work better for you and your family? For most of us, reading up on the healthcare system doesn't help clear our confusion. Much of what has been written about the problems of the US healthcare system are either human interest stories about individuals coping with debilitating illness or, at the opposite end of the spectrum, general gloom-and-doom statistics that highlight only troubling trends. Over the past several years, somewhat vague and sweeping predictions about the implications of the Patient Protection and Affordable Care Act (otherwise known as "healthcare reform") have frequently appeared in all forms of media, along with speculation as to whether some or all of the law will be repealed due to either a political changing of the guard or judicial review. There is very little written in the way of concrete solutions that can be systematically implemented, with or without government-driven reforms, and that the average person can understand and apply.

This book, unlike others lining bookstore shelves, is not about the alleged failings of our government and private-sector healthcare initiatives. Rather, it explains how our healthcare system works, why it has the flaws it has, and what can be done to improve it, regardless of which political party is in power or what laws are in effect. This book addresses the more than 250 million Americans[1] who are connected to organized systems of benefits and care through their health coverage and who, nonetheless, spend the majority of their lives confused and frustrated about how to navigate the US healthcare system.

My own experience with a serious chronic illness gave me an invaluable perspective on what it is like to be part of the US healthcare system, and it became one catalyst for me to try to make our healthcare system work better. At age nineteen, I was diagnosed with Crohn's disease, an incurable, often painful disease that causes, among other things, chronic inflammation of the digestive tract. While in my prime, I was told that I would likely spend several weeks a year in the hospital and might not be able to have a conventional career. For me, this prognosis created motivation instead of fear, and I tried to "outrun" both the pain of the disease and the prognosis. When my illness was diagnosed, I happened to be in college, studying management information systems. I was learning how to apply information and develop systematic approaches to different industries. As my career initially developed in the information systems consulting business, I was exposed to methods of applying systems science and information technology to solve complex problems in energy, mining, banking, manufacturing and distribution, pharmaceuticals, and healthcare delivery. I was fortunate to be at the forefront at a time when the application of information technology to improve business processes was starting to enter the mainstream. Ironically, just as I was determining to focus my career energies on the most complex of these industries—healthcare—my illness worsened and the two paths converged.

Beginning at age twenty-seven, and over the next seven years, I had seven abdominal surgeries, including the removal of my colon. During one of my hospital stays at a prestigious teaching hospital, in the span of forty-eight hours I was twice given medication to which I had a severe allergic reaction, even though my medical chart indicated that that particular drug should not be administered. Although some of the surgeries had positive outcomes, some did not. I experienced many of the flaws of the healthcare system, including poor coordination among providers, high cost, and in-adequate systems for communicating key information about medication allergies—a failure that sometimes proves fatal. As I navigated the system as a patient, even with my considerable professional experience in the industry at that time, it became clear how incomprehensible and inefficient our healthcare system was. However, it was equally evident that there was an abundance of excellent system components that made me feel very fortunate to be receiving my care in our country. I knew the resources being applied to help me were far less available, if available at all, in many other countries.

So, after implementing information management systems in multiple industries and serving as chief information officer (CIO) of several health-care payer organizations, some of which ran hospitals, clinics, and pharma-cies as well, I wondered why no one had yet applied a comprehensive, sys-tematic approach to healthcare. I decided to create a company with a mission to help enable a more capable and organized system of benefits and care.

My experience as a patient continues to inform my work, but it is the combination of that experience and my education and professional qualifi-cations that gives me what is perhaps a unique perspective. As a former CIO of healthcare payer and provider organizations and in my subsequent role as founding CEO and chairman of the board of the TriZetto Group, a healthcare information technology company that supplies solutions that link benefits and care for more than one hundred million people, I know the significant improvements that systematically applied technology can bring to the healthcare system. Today, at the age of forty-eight, I make sure my work stays informed by serving on the board of directors for Hoag Memorial Hospital Presbyterian; on the national board of the Crohn's and Colitis Foundation of America; and as an advisory member for the Center for Healthcare Policy and Research at the University of California, Irvine.

I have seen and continue to see firsthand the complex array of healthcare issues challenging patients, doctors, insurers, researchers, and others. Finally, my training in management information systems bolsters my ability to look at healthcare from a systems science point of view. This combined experience has compelled me to ask: How do all the parts of the healthcare system interact? And what is it about those interactions that perpetuates the poorly coordinated communication, lack of efficiency, and skyrocketing healthcare costs we are seeing today?

This book is intended to answer these questions in simple terms while also conveying that the problems of affordability and inefficiency plastering the headlines are absolutely solvable. You will see how other industries, such as retail and automotive manufacturing, have transformed their systems and how healthcare could benefit from similar approaches. Finally, since we are part of the system ourselves, this book will explore how we can improve our own healthcare experiences. We all need to play a more active role in making healthcare decisions based on cost and quality. And we need to start budgeting for healthcare much as we do for retirement, especially as employers shift more of the cost responsibility to consumers. But regardless of what we do, the system must be designed to give consumers like us better information with which to make healthcare decisions as well as to provide tools for saving, just as actively managed retirement plans help people save for retirement.

Any problem that is ignored, even if unintentionally, is likely to get worse. The key to taking action as a healthcare consumer is knowing how things work. Reading this book is an important step in understanding how the US healthcare system functions today and how it can and should be transformed.

For a sneak preview of what this transformation could look like by using an approach I call Integrated Healthcare Management (IHM), feel free to skip ahead to "Sarah's Story" beginning on page 155. Then, in order to understand how our system works now and the changes it must undergo for you to experience it as Sarah does, begin with chapter 1.

Chapter 1

Taking a Systems Approach

The whole is more than the sum of its parts.

—ARISTOTLE

D o not resuscitate. That is what some people think should be the fate of the US healthcare system. But is it truly beyond repair? When you read the newspapers, watch television, go to the Internet, or ask your neighbor, doctor, or pharmacist, you might think our healthcare system is among the worst in the world. Uncle Sam is often painted as an underperformer because the United States famously posts poorer longevity and higher infant mortality scores than other developed countries.

However, statistics don't tell the whole story. I, for one, do not believe these statistics are tabulated with equivalent levels of precision around the world. To begin with, the statistical playing field is not level. Because we operate with third-party payers (health insurance plans) that require highly accurate data for payment, we capture and report much more information than is captured in countries where doctors and other healthcare providers are paid a fixed salary. What is actually reported in those countries tends to make their healthcare systems look better than they would if more comprehensive data were reported.

Second, our most disenfranchised patients, whether citizens or not, tend to receive much of their healthcare in emergency rooms because they either cannot afford or do not have a primary care doctor. In addition, they forgo routine screenings and generally are not able to take care of healthcare needs as they arise. Instead, these individuals often seek care in the emergency room when their healthcare needs have become too serious to ignore. It so happens that US emergency rooms are one of the places where we capture statistical information with great precision and where both media attention and public interest often focus. When you combine patients who have received poor prior care with the high-cost setting of an ER, you get a skewed perspective on the US healthcare system.

Third, and more important than statistical precision or where statistics are gathered, is the substance of what we're measuring and reporting. Measuring and publicizing our country's healthcare system primarily by birth and death endpoints leaves out all the healthcare people get in between, which includes some of the best care in the world.

The reality is that many of the individual elements of the US healthcare system are in excellent shape—a fact that receives comparatively little press. We have highly trained physicians, nurses, and other medical professionals who are sought after by people in other countries as well as our own; we also have an abundance of first-rate medical facilities, state-of-the-art medical equipment technology, and effective and innovative drugs and other biotechnologies. But my point—and one of the main points of this book— is that the way in which the parts of the US healthcare system interact or fail to interact is the heart of the problem—not the medical care providers, not the insurance companies, not the relative amount of money spent on healthcare, not the pharmaceutical companies, or even the changes contained in healthcare reform legislation. Improving how the parts of the healthcare system work together makes sense regardless of healthcare reform legislation and whether or not it changes. We will see later in this book how an approach called Integrated Healthcare Management (IHM) can make all the parts of our healthcare system work together to reduce costs and improve quality through better sharing of information and better alignment of incentives. But first, let's examine what a system is and how our healthcare system in particular works.

Understanding the Systems Approach

What is a system? A system is a combination of elements and behaviors that interact to achieve an objective.

In order to improve our healthcare system, we first need to understand the components of that system and how they work together. So what is the US healthcare system anyway? Indeed, what is a system? It seems that systems are popping up everywhere—and not just in healthcare. We have transportation systems, food distribution systems, and even home entertainment systems. There is actually a discipline called systems science, although few people study it. The late C. W. Churchman, an esteemed professor at the University of California, Berkeley, from 1957 to 1996, was one of the first to define a "systems approach" to solving problems. While systematic thinking can and should include social policy, my experience is that when people throw up their hands and rely primarily upon policy intervention to solve a tough problem, it is usually due to a lack of systematic discipline. This is clear in the US financial system as well as in the healthcare system. And when crises occur, playing the blame game may make entertaining headlines, but it is not a path to systematically solving tough problems.

When you study systems, as I did in college, home heating is often the first concept you learn about. Understanding a simple closed system like this one is a good way to begin to understand systems science and—as we will see later—how systems science can be applied to fix the US healthcare system. The basic elements of a typical home heating system are the air in your home, the thermostat, and the furnace. The thermostat sets the target, measures the air temperature, and, if required, sends a signal to the furnace to heat and circulate the air. When the air reaches the desired temperature, the furnace shuts off. It's a simple and perfect closed system as long as you know what you want the temperature to be. Well, almost perfect.

However, suppose it's hotter outside than you want the temperature inside to be, and now you need to reduce the temperature inside your house. To do so, you need to add another element—the element of cooling—to the system. Now the thermostat has to be intelligent enough to tell the furnace when to go on or off, when to tell the air conditioner to go on or off, and when to tell both to do nothing. This is where many college students decide to study philosophy because they are smart enough to know that systems science only gets more complicated. For example, what about the air itself? How efficiently does it move around? What about humidity? Are the windows open? Should we cool the part of the house facing the sun and heat the part facing away from the sun to achieve the greatest efficiency? As you can see, designing a comprehensive heating and cooling system can become overwhelming if you consider every possible variable. So, whether you are designing a heating and cooling system or a system as massive as healthcare, it is important to focus your energy on the variables that matter most.

Systems Thinking Meets the Healthcare System

Many people think of the healthcare system as only the elements they can see and touch: the doctor's office, the hospital, and the local pharmacy. But as you will see, there is much more to the healthcare system than that. Even many doctors and other healthcare professionals do not understand all the elements of the healthcare system and how they affect one another. That is why assuming that your highly skilled physician is an expert concerning the entire healthcare system is similar to believing that your first-rate auto mechanic is an expert in the automotive and transportation industries. Most people intuitively know that even though their superstar mechanic has in-depth knowledge of particular makes and models of automobiles, and perhaps even specializes in transmissions, he or she is probably not qualified to run General Motors.

A similar analogy exists for doctors who become specialists. Specialists are systems experts on a subset of closed human systems, such as the digestive system, the circulatory system, or the nervous system. As advanced medical research yields deeper understanding of smaller and more discrete anatomical systems, specialists become even more specialized. And as these physicians expand their knowledge about treating patients within particular medical specialties, and even subspecialties within their specialties, they understandably have less time to focus on how the whole healthcare system ties together. Herein lies a paradox of systems thinking—and a problem in today's healthcare delivery system. If you have a medical problem involving the microscopic workings of your inner ear, then you probably are thankful there are specialists who pursue their understanding of the ear, nose, and throat system to the nth degree. But the fact that these specialists are able to solve your complex ear problem does not necessarily mean they understand the framework of the entire healthcare system. And from a systematic perspective, even if a well-researched and innovative treatment for your ear malady exists somewhere in the healthcare system, if your doctor does not know about it, or you cannot get access to this treatment because of your location, or if your health benefits plan doesn't cover it, that specialized knowledge is practically useless.

The Systematic Role of Primary Care Doctors

Fortunately, there are some physicians, typically called primary care doctors, who concentrate their careers on understanding how all the anatomical and certain psychological and social systems interact with and affect one another. These days, however, fewer and fewer medical students are choosing to become primary care doctors. Ironically, despite being trained to understand the whole human being both psychologically and physiologically, primary care doctors are not usually as well compensated as their specialized peers. From a systems science perspective, just as you cannot efficiently deploy the relatively advanced components of home heating and cooling systems without a thermostat, it is difficult to effectively deploy sophisticated components of the healthcare system (such as specialty care) without primary care doctors.

If the trend of more medical students choosing careers in specialty care continues, the United States could end up with the healthcare equivalent of too few "thermostats" to signal when the heating and cooling elements should go on and off. Primary care doctors are an essential control mechanism for the health of the patient, much the same way that thermostats are the control mechanism for the temperature of the house. Their understanding of the many variables that can affect the health of their patients qualifies primary care doctors to make smart decisions in consultation with their patients about when to "turn on" visits to specialists and other care settings beyond the primary care doctor's office.

For the house with no thermostat, the result might be either too high a temperature, wasting lots of expensive energy, or too low a temperature, which could cause the pipes to freeze and avoidable leaks to spring up. For the patient with no primary care doctor or accurate alternative information source, the result might be either too many unnecessary tests and visits to specialists and consequently an increase in healthcare costs, or not enough diagnostic tests or visits to specialists when these services are needed. In addition, the patient could spend more time in pain and run a greater risk that the illness or injury could become serious or, perhaps, deadly.

Addressing the shortage of primary care doctors is a difficult challenge. From a systems science perspective, we need to focus on the root causes of the problem. As we try to design a better healthcare system, how can we reverse the troubling trend of too few primary care doctors? Should we pay more to doctors who choose careers in primary care than to their specialist peers? Should we pay medical school tuition for those who commit to careers in primary care? Should we make the criteria for being accepted into such a tuition payment program very competitive so that we attract the best and brightest candidates to be our medical "thermostats" instead of becoming specialists? Some efforts are being made through healthcare reform legislation to create incentives to address the primary care shortage, such as student loan repayment programs and funding for training and education for primary care physicians and other professionals who practice in primary care. (We'll talk more about incentives and other solutions to our healthcare problems in chapter 8.) The good news here is that there is nearly universal agreement among all parties involved in the healthcare debate that access to primary care doctors is a crucial component of any improved system.

Clearly, primary care doctors (as well as specialists) play a central role in American healthcare. But it is important to realize that they represent only one element of the healthcare system—albeit a sacred one. Doctors and other providers have their hands full with the system elements they need to know in order to provide care to human beings. They cannot possibly know the whole healthcare system, and we should not assume they do.

Managing through Measuring: The Basics of Information Technology

So how do goal-seeking human beings today think about taming complex systems such as healthcare so they can better understand and manage them? The use of information technology can play an important role. Nearly anything that can be observed or measured that in turn would lead to a specified action (e.g., if the temperature is too low, then turn on the furnace) can be expressed as a mathematical or rules-based algorithm. The ability to capture measurements or values in digital form, process those data against a set of instructions or algorithms, and do something with the results is the backbone of modern information technology.

The world seems full of jargon about information technology, so let's make it easier to understand. "Software" is simply rules for operation, "hardware" simply determines how much data can be stored and how fast they can be processed, and "networks" simply determine both how quickly and where or to whom data can be transported. The challenge in information technology is assessing how best to use software, hardware, and networks to make specific objectives easier to achieve. In healthcare information technology, examples can range from deriving a clinical diagnosis that requires dozens of inputs with hundreds of permutations (for which even when assisted by a computerized diagnostic tool, the human brain of an experienced primary care physician is still the reigning supercomputer champion) to simple algorithms, such as a health plan checking whether a physician has entered a diagnosis code for an office visit or whether a prescription has been written and filled.

The press is full of stories about doctors being unfairly buried in administrative duties. However, before you express outrage that a physician should have to waste valuable time filling in a diagnosis code properly to get paid, keep in mind that failure to properly record a medication, test, or diagnosis could result in an allergic or adverse drug interaction, the unnecessary duplication of a particular test, or a delayed or incorrect diagnosis for that doctor's patient. And so, if you begin to think about it systematically— a habit I hope you will pick up from this book—administrative data used in the context of receiving accurate payment can also be used as important data for determining treatment of a patient in a clinical setting, such as a doctor's office or hospital. If you need medical care and the doctor treating you does not know about your past tests, diagnoses, and medications, you might wish the doctor had access to your health history in a digital (i.e., computer-accessible) form so she could see all the care you have received.

Information Underload

A wealth of data are being captured every day about who gets what healthcare and how much it costs. However, because these data are fragmented and much of the more insightful information is captured manually (instead of digitally) on those long paper forms you fill out every time you go to the doctor or in doctors' handwritten notes, it is not being used in the most timely or effective way, nor is it shared among the different parts of the healthcare system in order to help it run effectively. Stories abound about people ill on vacation receiving a drug to which they are allergic, simply because the information about the drug allergy was locked up in a paper-based file at their physician's office instead of being available where patients and providers need it.

Similarly, if you move to a new city or simply switch doctors, your medical record is not automatically transferred, and when it is, it's often in the form of manila folders stuffed with nonstandard forms in messy handwriting. As a result, your new provider has no practical way of knowing anything about your medical history, medications, allergies, past diagnostic tests, or risk factors unless you remember to include every detail on the new provider's paper form. This lack of information can lead doctors to order tests that have already been done, prescribe medication that can interact negatively with others you are taking, and cause countless other problems ranging from mere inconvenience or unnecessary expense to a dangerous drug interaction or misdiagnosis. However, this type of information deficiency is neither the doctor's fault, nor is it yours. The system was never engineered to assemble and distribute information to the greatest benefit of providers and patients.

Much is being made of the electronic health record as an answer to some of the information issues in our healthcare system. In fact, many doctors are converting to electronic or digitized medical records, and some are already using them. The American Recovery and Reinvestment Act of 2009 made funds available to providers who create electronic health records and use them in a meaningful way in their practices,[1] and that is a step in the right direction. (In chapter 9, we'll examine the differences among several types of computerized health records.) However, while having clear, legible, and accessible health records is important, you and your doctor should be wary of claims that the implementation of electronic health records alone will dramatically improve care or save money. Merely computerizing a flawed process speeds it up but does not fix it. In the information technology world, there is even a name for digitizing a system that is not well engineered to begin with: it is proverbially known as "paving cow paths." In order to make a tool such as the electronic health record more useful in improving care and saving money, technology and processes must be engineered together. For example, what if your handwritten health record were not only converted into an electronic health record, but in addition, it could enable your doctor to connect electronically to the prescription drug information that your health plan (insurer) stores in its own system? Now suppose that when you entered the exam room, instead of your doctor asking you to list the prescriptions you were taking, she were able to tell you the names of those prescriptions on record and simply ask you to verify the information? Here, technology would save your doctor time and give her more information than was contained in your original handwritten health record. A "cow path" would not be simply paved over in its original crooked form; rather, it would be straightened out and widened to make everyone's life easier. There are many immediate and practical ways in which information technology can be integrated with changes in processes throughout the healthcare system. In chapter 8, we will explore this powerful combination in more detail.

Coordination among System Parts

The nice thing about systems that are truly understood is that the major elements do not change. What can change, however, is our knowledge of what elements compose the whole system and the way in which those elements interact and coordinate with one another. That is where the potential for improvement lies. In a well-designed, well-engineered, and well-organized system, the whole should be greater than the sum of its parts.

A well-designed system should yield better results than you would get from any individual piece because the parts work together in a systematic way to create synergy. Let's use a trip to Las Vegas as an example. The fact that you can hop in your car and go to Las Vegas (assuming you live on the mainland) is the sum of a transportation system that links various parts in an organized way. Some of the major system elements are roads and the people who build them, cars and the people who make them, gas stations and the people who work in them, oil-producing countries and the entities that refine oil into gasoline, and people and companies who sell food so you can eat along the way.

As a consumer, you can navigate this system smoothly, so it is easy to take it for granted. Because of the way the parts work together, you can do exactly what you need to do when and how you choose to do it. The system as a whole allows you to accomplish more than if you simply experienced just one part of the system, such as driving in your car (but not being able to eat dinner or stop at a restroom along the way) or eating at a restaurant (but not having a car or a road to get you to Las Vegas). However, what if instead of being made of smoothed asphalt or concrete, all roads leading to Vegas were train tracks but your car still had four rubber tires? Not only would the road and your car not be designed to go together, but they would actually end up working against each other. Of course, this example would occur only if the railroad company owned all the land routes to Vegas and the mere notion of cars threatened its survival.

Ludicrous as it may seem, this is how parts of the US healthcare system are currently designed. Although many of the individual parts are excellent, the system as a whole is less than the sum of those parts. At the most fundamental level, there is poor communication among the parts of the system. Information is not shared among the various elements to allow them to get what they need when they need it, and much of the information exists in paper form instead of systematically being entered into a computer so it can be shared in digital form. To make matters worse, many of the healthcare system's well-intended financial incentives and penalties end up rewarding the wrong behaviors and do not encourage behaviors that would lead to better health, better treatment, and fewer dollars spent. Expecting our healthcare system to yield high-quality care at a lower cost without carefully designing the individual parts of the system to work together toward common goals is much like expecting that a car with rubber tires running on a train track will get you to Vegas.

The System through a Wider Lens

So why have we failed to structure the US healthcare system so the interactions among the parts add value for those of us who use it? Why don't the parts work in harmony to take us smoothly down the healthcare highway to our intended destination? How can we take a systems science approach to solving the problems of the US healthcare system? To begin with, systematically reengineering our healthcare system will require us to broaden our view of what is included in the system and to look beyond the doctor's office, the hospital, and the pharmacy. Let's take some examples of things we do every day. Is going to the grocery store part of the healthcare system? What about your daily hygiene and exercise routine? Is taking time off from work for a vacation part of the healthcare system? How about looking up generic healthcare information online? All of these behaviors can have a major influence on our health, yet few of us think of them as part of an organized healthcare system.

How about your health plan benefits? Are they part of the healthcare system? When you fill out the enrollment form for your health plan each year, do you think about how your choice of benefits will affect how much you pay for care as well as which providers you can see? If you get healthcare coverage through an employer (who pays the majority of the premium cost) or through the government, it's possible to take it for granted and feel entitled to receive health benefits. We might not think of the benefit plan as part of the healthcare system if access to this healthcare coverage has always been provided to us. But it is an important piece and one we need to think about carefully because the specific benefit plan we choose (or are assigned) is the organizing framework that affects both our cost and our quality of care.

Taking a systems approach means we need to have the most complete picture possible of all the parts of the system, and then we must structure the interactions among the parts to give everyone who uses the system what they need. One way to look at the healthcare system is to think of it in terms of the types of data collected throughout it. There are three primary groups of data that can be turned into useful systematic information about you as a consumer or about other parts of the healthcare system, such as providers (doctors and other healthcare professionals) and other users of the healthcare system (employers and brokers). The three primary groups contain data about benefits (called "core benefit administration"), data about how medical care should be managed and delivered (called "care management"), and data about specific characteristics and preferences you or others may have (called "constituent information").

The first group of data—core benefit administration—is information related to what most of us think of as the main business of insurance companies. This group of data comes from the health plans' processes of enrolling members, making contracts with doctors and hospitals regarding payment amounts for specific medical services, paying doctors and pharmacies for approved services they have performed (claims), and answering questions about coverage and other issues (customer service). The second group of data—care management—is information intended to help you receive high-quality healthcare. It includes care guidelines for treating you based on the "best practices" or most effective treatment for your condition or illness, rules the health plan has for what care can be provided by which type of provider and in which setting in order to be covered, and certain printed and online health information to help you and your doctor make informed healthcare decisions. The third group of data—constituent information—is information unique to each consumer or to providers, employers, and brokers, who are the other constituents in the healthcare system. Constituent information includes demographics (such as age and gender), preferences for how information is communicated (by phone, online, or by mail), whether prescriptions are in pill or liquid form, which pharmacy a patient uses, and other volunteered information that facilitates constructive interaction among healthcare constituents, particularly between providers and consumers (such as what language a consumer or provider speaks).

In most geographic areas, it is health plans that today are best positioned to coordinate these three types of information groups systematically so that information is shared. In certain geographic areas, integrated provider delivery systems are equally well positioned to facilitate the same type of coordination. In the context of healthcare reform, you are increasingly likely to hear about other types of organizations that are being formed to systematically coordinate healthcare information in order to cost-effectively improve the quality of care. The most notable newer examples are the Accountable Care Organization (ACO) and the patient-centered medical home (PCMH). (We'll learn more about these terms in later chapters.) With all the acronyms flying about the media, it is hard not to feel overwhelmed. However, the important thing to keep in mind is that increasingly, healthcare leaders are realizing that your health benefits, your care, and your preferences and characteristics need to be systematically considered and coordinated if we are to straighten out the cow paths.

Integrated Healthcare Management Is Key

Contrary to the pessimistic tone adopted by the media and politicians, the ills of the US healthcare system are eminently curable if we treat them systematically. I call this systematic view Integrated Healthcare Management (IHM), and I will explain it in detail in chapter 8 once I have more thoroughly covered how the healthcare system works now. IHM takes the best knowledge we have for managing benefits and the best knowledge we have for managing care and systematically coordinates both sets of knowledge in an optimal way for the healthcare consumer and the others involved with the system. If we can make the right information available wherever and whenever consumers, providers, employers, and brokers need it, and if we carefully craft behavioral incentives for people at every level of the system, we can reduce costs, improve quality, and make our healthcare system an example for the rest of the world. In other words, the US healthcare system may not be on the brink of failure, but rather on the brink of unparalleled success.

The first step in improving a system is to understand why it doesn't work. In chapter 2, "The Blind Men and the Elephant: Lessons for Healthcare," we will see the sheer immensity of the US healthcare system and why experiencing and understanding the entire system has been challenging for doctors, patients, and policy makers.

Chapter 2

The Blind Men and the Elephant:
Lessons for Healthcare

The wise man laughed as he turned and walked home. For he, himself, had once been as foolish as the others, thinking he knew what an elephant was like by simply touching one of its parts.
                    —FROM THE PARABLE "THE BLIND MEN AND THE ELEPHANT"

Understanding how the US healthcare system works is a monumental task. Its vast scale and tremendous complexity have baffled rocket scientists and brain surgeons alike. The sheer size of the healthcare system is mind-boggling. We have more than 815,000 doctors[1] in the United States. More than 5,700[2] hospitals throughout the country handle roughly 37.5 million admissions per year.[3] More than 3.6 billion prescriptions[4] were bought in 2009 from the roughly 2,100 commonly prescribed pharmaceuticals on the market.[5] In addition, more than three billion medical claims are processed each year.[6] Americans spent $2.5 trillion on healthcare in 2009, accounting for 17.3 percent of the gross domestic product during that year.[7] Given these numbers, it is no surprise that the average consumer has, at best, a cursory understanding of only a few parts of this enormous system. Add to these figures the amount of time, energy, and expertise involved in developing and managing all the parts of the system, and it's no wonder our healthcare system is so hard to figure out. Policy makers could spend all their time trying to understand how the entire system works, but they don't have that luxury. Instead, they must balance healthcare with the many other important issues on their plates; as a result, their understanding of the healthcare system is necessarily limited.

Yet understanding the whole system is the first step toward systematically engineering it to improve quality while lowering costs and toward helping the system to better serve you and your family.

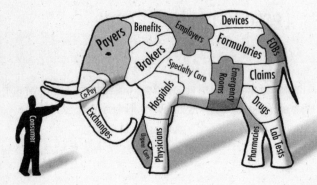

The well-known parable of the blind men and the elephant illustrates the impossibility of any person's getting to know the entire healthcare animal. This ancient metaphor has many different versions, but the basic story is this:

There once was a walled-in city where all of the inhabitants were blind. One day, a king stopped by with his entourage and camped on the outskirts of the city. He was accompanied by a large elephant, which he used to frighten his enemies away. Six blind men—each regarded as highly knowledgeable among their people—hurried out to "see" what the elephant was like. The first man, upon feeling the elephant's trunk, said, "This creature is long like a snake." The second man accidentally collided with the elephant's broad side. He exclaimed, "This beast is like a big wall—smooth and strong." The third man was nearly skewered by the elephant's tusk. Grimacing in pain, he said, "This animal is pointy and sharp like a spear. I see why the king's enemies keep their distance!" He ran away in fright. The fourth blind man reached down and found the elephant's leg, which was rough and dimpled. At that moment, the elephant stomped his foot, sending the blind man flying. The man said, "This elephant is like a moving tree trunk. It strikes the ground with a mighty force." Off he ran to join the others. The fifth man grabbed at the elephant's tail. "This animal can't scare anyone away. It is merely a frayed piece of rope." He walked off casually toward the city. The sixth man rushed out to see what the excitement was about. He felt the elephant's thin ear flapping in the breeze. "Wow! This creature is delicate just like a fan," he exclaimed.

Finally, a truly wise man came and walked slowly around the elephant, taking his time and studying the elephant thoroughly from all sides. He touched every part of it, listening to its sounds and smelling the elephant. After finding its mouth and feeding it a treat, he returned to the city. There he discovered the six blind men arguing about what the elephant was like. "It's like a snake," said one man. "No, it's like a wall," said another. "It's sharp like a spear," said a third man. "No, it's like a tree trunk," retorted another man. "No, it's like a rope," insisted another. "It's like a fan," said the last man. The wise man laughed as he turned and walked home. For he himself had once been as foolish as the others, thinking he knew what an elephant was like by simply touching one of its parts.

Feeling Our Way in the Dark

Think of the healthcare system as a huge elephant with each body part a different element, such as doctors, pharmaceutical companies, hospitals, pharmacies, medical equipment, consumers (patients), brokers, employers, and payers (the insurance companies that collect premiums and pay claims). Although most of us are not literally blind as in the parable, it often seems as if we are feeling our way through a dark jungle where our ability to fully see and comprehend the huge healthcare beast in front of us is severely impaired. Like the blind men in the parable, we as consumers each experience only small parts of the whole healthcare system—and solely in the narrow context of our own interactions. The result is a myopic view, rather than a thorough, systematic understanding of all parts of the US healthcare system and how they interact with one another.

Here's an example: Imagine meeting the healthcare beast for the first time, perhaps in your first job. This encounter may be through an employer during an open enrollment period (or, if you are self-insured, directly through your health plan). Like the blind men, you touch this part of the healthcare animal and form an impression. You might perceive the healthcare system as a long form you must complete; choices you must make about what benefits, doctors, and hospitals you will be able to access; and a big, fat payroll deduction about to gobble up your hard-earned paycheck. But missing from your picture of the healthcare system are many other pieces of information, such as the cost of each procedure or test you need during the year or throughout your lifetime, how the hospitals and networks of doctors run their businesses, and how brokers may advise your employer about which health plan and group of benefits it should offer. You also may not have realized how the parts of the system are connected. For example, when you filled out the enrollment form at your first job, did you think about the fact that if you had to switch employers someday, you'd likely have to switch health plans, which might mean leaving the doctors you know and trust?

Once enrolled in the health plan, you would typically make an appointment with your primary care doctor. From this interaction, you might begin to see the healthcare system as a provider of basic care, a source of information, a giver of referrals to specialists, and a place to read hours' worth of magazines you would ordinarily never pick up. However, there is much of the healthcare system you still can't see, such as whether the doctor or nurses know anything about you before you enter the exam room, how your doctor is paid by the health plan for the care you receive, the network of hospitals and diagnostic centers with which your physician is affiliated, the criteria your doctor will use to decide if you need a referral to a specialist, and the list of approved drugs your health plan will cover (called a formulary).

As you venture further into the healthcare system, the jungle around you seems to become darker and darker. You play a bit too much tennis one weekend and return to work with a case of tennis elbow. You try to find a specialist for your elbow, but you struggle to get an appointment. You finally track down an orthopedist who has an available appointment within this decade. When you arrive at the orthopedist's office, you are told that your referral from the primary care doctor was not received and you will need to sign a coverage waiver and pay for the visit out of pocket. After reading more magazines, you are led into an exam room where the specialist examines you for a period of time much briefer than your wait. The doctor then asks the nurse to prepare an order for you to receive an MRI (magnetic resonance imaging) test, which allows a doctor to see high-definition pictures of the inner workings of your elbow, just to be sure something more serious is not in play. After you go to the diagnostic center for your MRI, having read still more magazines (which is OK because you can't have your mobile phone on), you are able to arrange a follow-up appointment with the orthopedist with amazing efficiency compared to your first visit. The physician rules out a more severe diagnosis that would have required surgery, and he develops a treatment plan with physical therapy and prescriptions for painkillers and anti-inflammatory medications. You now perceive the healthcare system as a long search for a specialist, poor communication between your doctor's office and the specialist's office, an obligation to pay for care that should have been covered, an interminable wait to see the specialist, a professional but very short examination, a visit to a diagnostic center, an efficient follow-up visit, a referral for physical therapy, and—at long last—prescriptions to alleviate your symptoms.

Size and Complexity Challenge Consumers

By now, you have interacted with several different parts of the healthcare animal: your employer, your primary care doctor, and now this specialist. You may think you are developing quite a comprehensive image of the healthcare system. But what you don't see is the complexity of orthopedics or of specialty care in general. You saw a general orthopedist, but there are also orthopedists who specialize in hip or knee replacements, others who specialize in hands and fingers, and so it goes for many parts of the body except, perhaps, a broken eyelash. There are nearly 150 medical specialties and subspecialties. If orthopedics alone is so complex and specialized, imagine how difficult it would be for anyone to know the whole healthcare system or even to understand all that relates to the delivery of care alone. As we learned in chapter 1, the healthcare system comprises not only delivery of care but also benefits administrators (health plans or payers) as well as the individuals, or constituents, who use the system—consumers, providers, employers, and brokers. Even with the interactions you have accumulated, you have barely scratched the surface of the healthcare system's complexity.

As you advance deeper into the dark jungle, you see other parts of the healthcare elephant. For example, when you fill your prescriptions at the local pharmacy, you start to view the healthcare system as a collector of co-payments, a giver of the medication your doctor prescribed, and maybe even a provider of instructions on when to take the drug. But you don't see the complex research and development organ inside the healthcare animal, which invented, tested, and brought your drugs to market. It is also unlikely that you know the actual retail cost of the drugs you receive because you pay only a small fraction (your co-payment) of the total cost. And while you are waiting for your prescriptions, you are probably unaware that the pharmacist is checking your eligibility (whether your health plan covers these particular prescription drugs) and your co-payment amount with a computer database from your health plan or the pharmacy benefit manager hired by the health plan. In this situation, you never experience the parts of the elephant responsible for paying for most of your prescription—the health plan and the employer. Like the blind men, you see only one part of the whole.

Consumers also may have very different impressions about the healthcare system because their interactions even with the *same* part of the system may vary. For example, if you have a mail-order prescription benefit and your prescription doesn't arrive at your house on time, you may view the healthcare system as an inefficient, bureaucratic impediment to getting the medicine you need. However, if your prescription appears on your doorstep right when you expect it, you'll probably think the healthcare system is a well-oiled machine that just saved you a trip to the pharmacy. Such is the result when people think of one small part or one limited interaction as the whole system.

Seeing the Whole System: Is It Possible?

We've seen how consumers develop a narrow view of the healthcare system from touching only a few parts of the whole. Similarly, the *other* parts of the system, such as doctors, physician assistants, nurses, physical therapists, pharmacists, hospital professionals, and employers also touch only a few other parts of the system and can also be likened to the blind men in the parable. And while any one of these parts of the healthcare system may be an expert in its own processes and procedures, each knows little about the rest of the system, and some have no idea the other parts exist. For example, your pharmacist interacts with patients, doctors, hospitals, and payers, but he may never touch the brokers or employers. And his experiences with the parts he does touch are limited. He sees patients as receivers of medications, the health plan as the giver of permission, and the doctor (and other providers) as an authorized entity that orders prescriptions, but he never sees these parts in their entirety as they relate to one another.

Similarly, while your primary care doctor may be an expert in internal medicine, if you need surgery or have a heart problem, cancer, or an issue with your lungs or your endocrine system, your doctor will probably need to refer you to a specialist. Just learning internal medicine took years of medical school, an exhausting internship and residency, and years of experience treating patients. Despite this arduous training, it would be unreasonable to expect your doctor to be an expert in every specialty or to have as thorough an understanding of the other parts of the elephant, especially those she may never touch directly, such as employers, brokers, and payers.

As with the blind men trying to get a complete understanding of the elephant but describing it in entirely different ways, we, too, may think we fully understand the healthcare system based on repeated encounters with one small part, or even several. However, the healthcare system simply has too many parts, each of which is too large and complex for every part to fully know all of the others. Because of the immensity and complexity of the US healthcare system, it is virtually impossible for any patient or provider to understand it as one organism. And why should people try to understand a whole system when what they really care about is whether their own interactions with the system give them what they need?

We all know the US healthcare system is not performing up to its full potential. However, until we consistently start to treat healthcare as a system, in its true definition, with knowledge of all the parts and how they work together, we will not be able to tame this unruly beast and get it to do what we need it to do. Up to now, much energy has been focused on trying to fix whatever part of the system policy makers perceive as the biggest problem at any given time. But this approach leaves out the interactions among the parts. Improving just one part of the system without considering how the other parts interact will not necessarily make the system work more efficiently, any more than constructing a state-of-the-art train track would help the car with rubber tires in chapter 1 move from one place to another.

When Is a System Really a System?

By the time you finish this book, you will have a basic understanding of the parts of the US healthcare system. You will also know that in most areas of the country, healthcare is not an organized system at all. In order to successfully navigate the healthcare jungle, you need to understand that the system is disconnected and that often there is no one person or entity making sure you get all the care and information you need. In other words, there is no healthcare equivalent of the wise man in the fable (although there are some entities striving to become wiser). Simply knowing that no single entity completely understands the system should make you realize that you need to become a more active participant in your own healthcare. Only then can you seek the most effective elements of the system with the best efficiency and results.

> **Looking at how other industries have successfully engineered or reengineered their systems to achieve the best possible outcome may shed light on our attempt to improve the US healthcare system. In chapter 3, we will travel down the road with one automotive company that successfully applied technology and systems engineering principles to create a state-of-the-art system for production, care, and maintenance while delivering higher quality for less cost. Sadly, this is a feat that our healthcare system has yet to accomplish on any broad scale for humans.**

Chapter 3

The Lexus and the Human

It's a very funny thing about life; if you refuse to accept anything but the best, you very often get it.

—W. SOMERSET MAUGHAM, "THE TREASURE," 1940

Which would you rather be: a Lexus® or a human being? The answer may seem obvious. A human enjoys free will, the pursuit of happiness, and many other privileges we hold dear, while the Lexus is simply a car at the mercy of whoever ends up in the driver's seat. But if you have ever seen how easily a Lexus is able to be "treated" for an "illness" and how thorough and transferable its communications-linked maintenance records are in comparison to the fragmented paper-based medical records at your doctors' offices, you might just opt to be a Lexus.

In 1992, I purchased a Lexus LS400®. At the time, Lexus advertised that no matter which Lexus dealer you took your car to for service, that dealer would know about you and how to take care of your car because the service records from all Lexus dealers were linked through a satellite network. Given my interest in systems engineering and information technology, I was intrigued by this pioneering attempt to systematize how routine service and repairs were tracked and provided. Also, because I had done information systems consulting work in the manufacturing industry, I was curious as to whether the company's claims of applying information technology to improve both the ownership experience and the driving experience held up in reality.

To my delight, the advertising claims were actually true. Despite the fact that the Internet was not commonly used by the general public in 1992, Lexus had made use of the best technology available at the time for this application—satellite-linked networks—and used it to give consumers and dealers the information they needed where and when they needed it. Further, Lexus had built information sensors into the car itself that, when connected to the network by technicians, could help diagnose and fix problems when they occurred. To this day, any Lexus dealer can access the service record of any Lexus and see which services have been performed and whether the Lexus needs an oil change, is due for a 75,000-mile checkup, or could use a brake replacement. Lexus was the first in its field to implement this type of standardized service system across locations. Unsurprisingly, it fast became the standard for the automotive industry.

Lexus links information for repair and maintenance . . .

Lexus's communications-linked maintenance system not only works well for the owner of the Lexus (the consumer), but also gives the authorized service technician (the provider) valuable information he can use to best service the car. The technician is prompted as to which services to perform for a routine maintenance checkup, and he treats the Lexus based on standard established practices for a car model of that particular Lexus's condition and age. Once those services are performed, the technician electronically records exactly what was done so next time the car needs repairs, any certified Lexus technician will be able to pick up where the last person left off. When the car needs repairs (has an illness or injury), the technician can see which diagnostic procedures have already been done, thereby avoiding unnecessary duplication or waste such as changing the oil twice in three months. The technician also has access to information about the Lexus's warranty (analogous to health insurance coverage for a human), allowing both the car owner and the dealer to know up front which services the car owner will have to pay for out of pocket and which will be covered. This means the service technician is also able to give an accurate pricing estimate before work is performed and an accurate bill when the work is completed. Finally, the Lexus has a proactive reminder system for letting a Lexus owner know when to take the vehicle in for routine maintenance such as an oil change.

. . . while fragmentation plagues human care.

In stark contrast to Lexus's systematic way of maintaining and repairing its cars, the US healthcare system lacks the coordination to care for humans as reliably and comprehensively. Although the human race has been around much longer than the Lexus, and even though a luxury automobile is an inanimate object, the Lexus enjoys a much higher degree of precision regarding its care. For starters, our system does not reliably enable providers and consumers to access medical records wherever and whenever we need them. Each doctor's office keeps information relating only to that doctor's treatment of a particular patient, and in most cases, it is handwritten, so it can't be transmitted easily to another doctor or hospital. As a result, the same diagnostic tests are often performed unknowingly by different doctors on the same patient, driving up the cost of medical care and wasting the patient's time. In some cases, this lack of record availability can lead to more serious consequences. As I mentioned earlier, if you are unconscious and are delivered by ambulance to an emergency room, the doctors and nurses might inadvertently give you a drug to which you are allergic because they can't access your medical record. To add insult to injury, once you are released from the emergency room, there is no guarantee that documentation of the treatment you just received will be sent to your primary care doctor to be entered into your medical record.

Not only are we humans unable to access our medical records when needed, there is also a tremendous degree of variation in the treatment we receive, even among people with the same conditions and similar health backgrounds. Treatment of humans, unlike the Lexus, is not consistently based on "best practices" (the treatment that research has shown to be most effective for a particular condition given a patient's age, overall health, and family history of disease). Studies show that although healthcare experts have researched and documented best practices for a wide variety of medical conditions, patients often receive treatment that is different from what is proven to be most effective. This difference between the best practice and another form of treatment a patient receives is referred to as "unwarranted variation." It is the root of deficiencies in quality and inefficiencies in cost and can have severe, sometimes deadly, implications for patients. For example, there is agreement within the medical community that, following a heart attack, patients who can tolerate them should be given beta blockers (a class of pharmaceutical drugs) to lower the risk of recurrence. Yet even though this practice is almost as basic a step as making sure the oil filter is replaced during an oil change, it is not followed consistently. In fact, one landmark study in 1995 (three years after I bought my Lexus) showed that between 5 percent and 93 percent of heart attack patients—depending on the patient's provider—were given the beta blockers.[1] How would you like to be one of the patients whose doctor was unaware of this well-researched and inexpensive treatment protocol or was under the false belief that it wasn't important? Can you imagine this level of variation on the assembly line of a high-end automobile manufacturer? And further, in a question to be raised later in this book, should doctors who don't adhere to established best practices be reimbursed differently from those who do?

The fact that such a high degree of unwarranted variation exists in healthcare is a disturbing thought—as well as a reason for optimism. We all know that doctors in the United States receive rigorous medical education and years of practical training before they are licensed to practice medicine. They are constantly deepening their technical knowledge and broadening their experience caring for patients. Given the training and experience of American doctors, it was quite an eye-opener in the 1990s when Dr. Jack Wennberg first brought to light this unwarranted variation in treatment. In research published in the Dartmouth Atlas of Health Care, Wennberg found variation in the way chronically ill people were treated from one part of the country to another and that the treatment was directly related to the availability of medical services in particular geographic areas. He also uncovered variations in the rates of knee replacements, heart surgeries, and other surgical procedures, which he attributed to differences in opinion among doctors about whether surgery should be performed over nonsurgical treatments.[2] The reason I say there is cause for optimism given these disturbing findings is that this unwarranted variation in the way patients are treated for the same condition is one area where we have tremendous potential to improve the healthcare system. After all, as I said earlier, most of our doctors are highly trained, well-intentioned professionals. Certainly, the fact that they treat similar conditions in different ways has something to do with whether and how the ever-changing body of best practice (or evidence-based) information is made available to doctors throughout the country. Just as important as how this information is shared with doctors is how quickly and how consistently it is incorporated into practice once doctors know these guidelines.

There are other reasons for the levels of unwarranted variation in the care we humans receive. Dr. Atul Gawande, a prominent surgeon at the Brigham and Women's Hospital in Boston, identified an extremely simple solution to some of the unwarranted variation in healthcare: checklists. In his best-selling book *The Checklist Manifesto: How to Get Things Right*, Dr. Gawande shows how using a tool as basic as a checklist of essential tasks can mean the difference between life and death or between a quick recovery and an extended (and more expensive) hospital stay. Gawande makes the point that the amount and complexity of the information that providers must know is so great that they need tools (even ones as straightforward as checklists) to help them deliver the right care consistently and safely.[3] Whether the answer is checklists, better delivery to doctors of the latest best practice information, or other ways to reduce the variation we humans experience, we need to bring the level of consistency in our healthcare at least to the level of care that the Lexus receives—and hopefully much higher than that.

The Lexus's care not only is more consistent than that of humans, but the warranty (or in the case of humans, the coverage) is better. In contrast to the Lexus's easily available warranty that shows both consumers and dealers which services are covered, in our healthcare system the providers do not always know what services are covered for their human patients, nor do they know how much these services cost. For example, if your doctor decides you should see a specialist and gives you a list of three specialists who have impeccable reputations, she probably does not know which of those doctors may be available to you at a lower cost because they are in your health plan's approved network. After all, the doctor is there primarily to diagnose and treat you, not to manage your healthcare benefits. Nor does the doctor's front desk staff necessarily have the most up-to-date list of which specialists are in your health plan's network (although they almost always know if they themselves are accepting a negotiated rate from your health plan). If you don't know how to find out if the specialist is in your network, then you could inadvertently end up paying more money out of pocket than if you had gone to another excellent specialist on the list who happens to be in your health plan's approved network.

Doctors are not the only ones with incomplete information about your health insurance coverage. Patients often only know the co-payment amount instead of the total cost of a given procedure, so they might conclude that a visit to the family doctor or having the dermatologist remove a mole only costs fifteen dollars instead of the actual (and much higher) cost of this care. Moreover, many people are unaware of the large monthly contribution employers pay toward the health insurance premium; consequently, they might be lulled into believing that health insurance only costs the amount they pay per month, instead of that amount plus their employer's larger contribution. As you will see in later chapters of this book, if we don't know the total cost of care we are receiving, then we cannot make informed decisions about whether the care we receive is worth the money we are being charged, nor can we ever hope to reduce our healthcare costs.

Finally, humans, unlike the Lexus, generally do not have a reliable reminder system for scheduling checkups and screening tests. And in general, physicians do not have easy access to the most up-to-date guidelines for how often a particular patient should have various screenings and checkups based on that individual's gender, age, health status (how sick or healthy a patient is), family history, and risk factors for disease. Without these measures in place to ensure consistency, the best that many people can hope for is to receive a checkup reminder card in the mail that they had self-addressed at their last appointment. And far too few humans are ever automatically reminded to have their cholesterol checked, their annual Pap smear done, or other routine screenings performed. When we consider how important prevention is and its powerful role in increasing longevity, it is inexcusable that our human healthcare system is so far behind the Lexus in this regard.

Japanese Manufacturing: The Whole Becomes Greater Than the Sum of Its Parts

Toyota, the parent company of Lexus, was one of several Japanese car man-ufacturing companies to revolutionize the automobile industry in the 1980s and early 1990s. While Lexus stood out as a premium brand in its ability to use technology to deliver customized care and improve commu-nication among Lexus technicians everywhere, the transformation of the automobile industry as a whole took place at two different levels. Before Japanese car companies could get to the level of customized services and satellite-linked information, they first had to step back and take a broad look at their design, manufacturing, and distribution processes and connect the disjointed elements so they could work as a complete, efficient system. The Japanese did not merely improve the speed of their assembly lines or throw more money at fixing the one piece of the manufacturing system they perceived to be the weakest. Instead, they approached this challenge sys-tematically, carefully examining the whole manufacturing, distribution, and customer service system from every angle to determine how each piece should work with the others to produce a distinctly higher-quality auto-mobile at a notably lower cost than anything comparable in its class.

Japanese automakers used systems science to reengineer their design, manufacturing, and distribution processes. Ironically, the principles they used were largely based on the work of W. Edwards Deming, an American who previously had been laughed out of Detroit. This disbelief in Deming's principles at the time warrants serious consideration in the context of this book. It simply did not make sense to US auto companies that you could produce a substantially higher-quality product at a substantially lower cost. After all, Cadillacs® and Lincolns® were expensive cars with luxurious mate-rials, and such luxury and comfort was viewed as *having* to cost more. Brand names commanded higher value; as long as you could sell at a suffi-ciently high price, you could increase the expense to deliver the goods, reasoned US automakers. And just imagine the gall of a self-proclaimed "efficiency expert" to tell Detroit automakers—who had created the largest product companies in the world—how to improve their businesses. Mean-while over in Europe, there was not only a strong emphasis on engineering superiority in automobile design, but also the general belief that such superiority should naturally cost more—in the case of Mercedes®, much more.

In the early 1980s, we had dominant brands such as Chevrolet®, Ford®, and Chrysler® producing automobiles with similar performance characteristics to one another and selling them for prices that US citizens had no choice but to accept. After all, people needed cars, and that was what they cost. Just choose your model based upon your socioeconomic status. And, of course, people got used to the price of a new model going up each year, along with the prices of gas, auto insurance, tires, and car repairs and maintenance. It was a seemingly perfect system and became the basis for entire regional economies. Consumers bought into the notion that in the category of automobiles, the price-performance curve was just the way things had to be. Does that behavior look familiar in the realm of US healthcare?

You don't have to delve too deeply into the manufacturing processes of that time to know that the US model of linear assembly lines, storing enormous amounts of inventory, and performing quality checks late in the manufacturing process after much of the work had been completed was the antithesis of what Japanese automakers were cooking up. The Japanese took a page out of the European book on superiority of engineering design, adding their own knowledge of electronics. They worked in small teams, checking quality early and often to minimize rework; they applied just-in-time concepts to avoid carrying expensive inventory; and they thought about how to extend their design and engineering specifications to distributors (auto dealers) for purposes of proactively maintaining the quality of their products even after delivery to consumers. As a result, Japanese automakers could design, build, and deliver automobiles faster and at a lower cost. Satisfaction among both customers and suppliers improved dramatically, and customer choice was enhanced by offering customization. Once US consumers got over their disdain for unfamiliar brands (and the Japanese ultimately learned how to create brand appeal), Japanese automakers gained significant market share because they were able to design much higher-quality cars more cost-effectively. And while I acknowledge competitive labor cost differences for US automakers (in part because of the comparatively higher cost of US healthcare), it is essential to understand that it was an overall change in systematic design on the part of the Japanese that set off the auto wars, with labor costs being one component of that system. In other words, the higher-quality-at-lower-cost curve demanded a new way—a better-engineered way—of process design.

Systematic Thinking Meets Applied Technology and Information Technology

Even if you are able to conceptualize a "better mousetrap" as Lexus did, it becomes an entirely different challenge to repeatedly produce high quality on a large scale. In other words, producing hundreds of thousands of automobiles and properly maintaining them, or managing tens of millions of healthcare consumers according to a series of best practices, is a herculean task. Fortunately, there are two types of technological advancements that help us humans accomplish things beyond our individual and collective capacity: applied technology and information technology.

It has often been said the definition of technology is "anything that didn't exist when you were born." It's hilarious but true. My grandparents couldn't work their VCR, my parents can't run their home theater system, and I struggle to manipulate the touch screen on my kids' mobile audio devices. Each of these examples illustrates *applied technology* (how technology can be used in a specific industry or product group—in this case, media). In the automotive industry I just described, some examples of applied technologies are new types of sound-damping steel and aluminum alloys, robotics used to repeat painting sequences with precision, and engineering design applied to shape a car to reduce its drag coefficient. In healthcare, examples of applied technologies are glucose meters for instantly measuring a diabetic's glucose level, the da Vinci® surgical robot that enables minimally invasive surgery, biotechnological innovations that produce pharmaceutical chemical compounds, and even stem cells that grow into replacement organs. Applied technology innovations are potentially infinite because they are ongoing. You would be hard-pressed to keep track of all the applied technologies for an industry as vast as either manufacturing or healthcare even if you were to read journals and articles all day, every day.

However, from a systems science perspective, as remarkable as these applied technology innovations are, they are just elements of the system and rarely provide the impetus for solving a problem regarding how an entire system such as healthcare works. For example, for twenty years I have listened to pundits explain how storing health records in a microchip embedded in a plastic ID card is the panacea for healthcare, or that the digital mobile phone is the answer to the problem of delivering healthcare information to the right place at the right time. These prognostications are made by people I refer to as "gadget freaks," who are usually in the business of selling gadgets. Doesn't it seem silly to consider carrying around a physical copy of your health records on a chip (which means your provider would have to have the gadget that can decode your chip) when secure Internet access is almost universally available? And as for the mobile phone, let's do a reality check on how many people can keep track of calls, voice messages, text messages, contacts, calendars, and MP3 music collections simultaneously before we assume that putting more information on the same gadget will not become merely another distraction. Nonetheless, applied technologies are often incredible, wonderful enablers of broader systematic designs.

Information technology is the second form of technology that helps humans systematically produce high quality on a scale as large as automobile manufacturing. Through information technology, the Japanese and, ultimately, US automakers were able to link design, manufacturing, and distribution processes in a systematic way so that each element showed up when and where it should. A computer in and of itself is really just a gadget. But when you add software (instructions) and data, you are beginning to enter the realm of information technology. And when you apply computing, software, and data and information management to automate the work of people as well as processes and applied technology, you have stepped into the world of enterprise information technology. Without enterprise information technology, transformation of the auto industry probably would not have occurred. Additionally, there would be no enterprises with the scale and efficiency of Walmart, nor would the United States have a functioning private health insurance industry serving hundreds of millions of people and a Medicare program serving tens of millions of people.

Shared Information: Right Place, Right Time!

During the late 1980s and into the 1990s, tremendous progress was made in the development of enterprise information technology solutions combining greater computing power with complex software capable of manipulating increasingly vast amounts of data. This progress continues today, and these innovations have important implications for how complex systems can apply information technology to manage information, goods, and services more efficiently. The automotive industry first drove the innovation of what were originally called manufacturing requirements planning or MRP systems. These software solutions enabled manufacturers to enter a product design, keep track of all the materials and processes required to build it, track each piece and part through a series of automated and human labor processes, and keep track of the finished goods. Early in my career, I had the chance to help develop and implement some of these early solutions, and it was a great background for thinking about how to tackle the challenges in healthcare. Those early systems have evolved into what are known today as enterprise resource planning or ERP systems and are used to precisely plan, schedule, and monitor every step in producing a good or service. The healthcare system has no equivalent way to plan, schedule, support, and monitor the care you receive.

Similarly, early attempts at automated distribution systems to track demand by and facilitate sales to end customers have developed into today's customer relationship management or CRM solutions, used by retail giants such as Walmart. Walmart uses information technology linked from each of its checkout registers to each of its suppliers to ensure that the thousands of products consumers purchase are continually available and that the price of these products is accurate and competitive. Both the automotive and retail industries have succeeded in combining information technology with well-designed systems—an effective combination.

Systems Approach and the Right Information Technology Can Transform Healthcare

So why have we not been able to make as significant inroads in solving the healthcare crisis as we have accomplished in the automotive, retail, and other industries? The information technology certainly exists to transform the healthcare system, but we first need to take a systematic approach to understanding and fixing the system. We are much like the automakers of the 1980s in that we have some excellent processes that function as independent entities. Some of the linear "assembly lines" in doctors' offices, insurance companies, benefits administration companies, hospitals, disease management companies, the pharmaceutical industry, and virtually every other area of the healthcare system are quite good at what they do. However, far too often each of these parts of the healthcare supply chain is like the blind men in the previous chapter—able to feel only its own part of the healthcare elephant and unable to see how the parts work together to form a complete system.

I am now on my second Lexus after giving my first one—which is still in great health for its age—to my mother. Each time I take it in for maintenance and witness the efficiency of the Lexus service system, I am struck by the contrast between the quality practices for the care of the Lexus and those for the human. I don't mean to imply by my comparison that servicing cars and caring for human beings share the same level of complexity; obviously the latter is a far more nuanced endeavor. However, there is simply no reason, given the information technology that exists, that we can't engineer the healthcare system to give human beings care that is coordinated, consistent, efficient, and based on the best practices available today.

In chapter 4, we will look at what composes the healthcare supply chain and how it is organized by both private payers and the federal and state governments. We will also examine supply chains in the auto and retail industries and see how the organizers of these supply chains attempt to balance supply and demand and add value to the system.

Chapter 4

Understanding the Healthcare Supply Chain

Chaos was the law of nature; Order was the dream of man.
—Henry Brooks Adams,
The Education of Henry Adams: An Autobiography, 1918

Suppose you are the owner of the Lexus® in the last chapter. How did you decide which type of car to purchase? Your decision may have been based on *Consumer Reports* ratings such as how many miles per gallon the car gets and how it performs on safety measures. You probably also considered cost, appearance, ergonomics, how the car handles, its size relative to your hauling needs, and available color options. If you were very knowledgeable, you may have researched whether the car has a communications-linked system for repairs and maintenance, how quickly it loses its value after purchase, and its total cost of ownership over a five-year life or its average cost per mile, assuming you will drive it for one hundred thousand miles.

Behind the Scenes: The Supply Chain

Once you decided on your Lexus, you probably compared prices from various dealerships and online sources before making your purchase. Although you may not have realized it at the time, when you bought your car, you bought not only the vehicle but also the value added by the car's *supply chain*—the designers, producers, parts and labor suppliers, storage facilities, transporters, distributors, and retailers that participate in the sale, production, and delivery of a particular product. In other words, from the time your car was designed, people and companies along the way provided their expertise in many areas, striving to enhance the value of the product so they would be paid proportionately for their contribution to its ultimate purchase price. They designed the car with an eye toward quality, style, and the outstanding service they know you deserve. In designing the car, they made sure recent technologies such as your daughter's MP3 player could plug into your car and play her favorite music and videos, that you could find your way using a satellite-assisted navigation system, and that you could use built-in hands-free Bluetooth® technology for your mobile communications. They selected only the finest sound damping and noncorrosive metals for manufacturing and negotiated a reasonable purchase price for these materials. They assembled the car according to established production engineering guidelines to ensure consistency and quality, and then they priced the car fairly while also eking out a profit. They established a network of dealerships where you could access the car for a test drive and seek help from trained and knowledgeable sales staff, and they transported your car from the manufacturing plant to the dealership. They inspected the car, making sure it had all the options you ordered and was clean and shiny, complete with a full tank of gas and even a fully charged hybrid battery when you drove it off the lot. They also reminded you about their communications-linked service system, bundled in your routine maintenance so you would keep visiting Lexus dealerships even if you moved, and offered you a discount on your first oil change. Finally, they programmed all the steps, from ordering your new car through production and delivery, into a computerized enterprise resource management system that could be accessed, updated, and tracked by all participants in the supply chain to ensure quality and timeliness.

Of course, not all cars you test drove impressed you quite like the one you selected. Maybe the price was too high for what you perceived the car was worth (possibly because the purchasers in that car's supply chain did not negotiate a good price for the materials they used). Or perhaps there were aspects of the design or quality that fell short. There are two points to be made about how you decided which car to buy and how this decision relates to healthcare:

First, each product or service you purchase has its own supply chain, which affects how you perceive its value—the features and level of quality you get for the price you pay.

Second, if you are not able to evaluate certain information to determine value when making a purchase, it is very difficult to match expectations to results. I have learned that most people determine value based upon whether a good or service meets or exceeds their expectation for the price they paid.

As I touched on in chapter 3, the ability of a typical consumer—you or me—to assess the value of services rendered in the US healthcare system is extremely limited. This is the case for a number of reasons, not the least of which is that historically, consumers have not known the total cost of the healthcare services they receive. For example, do you know whether a prescription drug you pick up at the pharmacy for ten dollars has a retail price of $439 or $4.99? We have gotten used to this phenomenon in healthcare, so it may seem perfectly normal; however, can you imagine a world where having automobile insurance entitles you to use a car anytime you want for a five-dollar co-pay? Not just when your car is in the shop, but every day? We will explore this issue later in the book, but it's important for any consumer to step back and systematically consider the elements of supply chain and value. Of course, this is best done when you are not in dire need of medical care, as it is a very rare person who can make value-based inquiries of his doctor or other members of the medical staff when lying unclothed under a paper gown, facing the anxiety of his own health challenges. Over the years, I have evolved into just such a creature, a fact my doctors tend to find entertaining. However, my hope is that as you read this book, you are in a more comfortable setting to think about the supply chain and to see the clear health and cost benefits of creating a truly integrated healthcare supply chain.

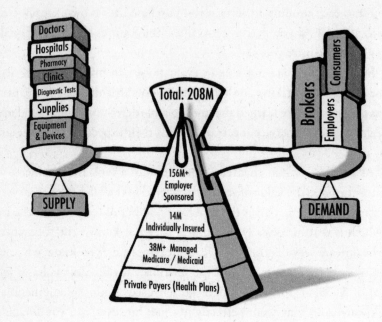

Elements of the Healthcare Supply Chain

The US healthcare system is a supply chain. There are many types of *suppliers* as well as several elements that create demand. If you look at the preceding figure,[1] you may recognize most of the suppliers listed on the left side of the scale, but you're probably less familiar with the demand elements on the right, and probably even less familiar with how health plans serve as supply chain managers in the middle. By the end of this chapter, your understanding of all these elements should help you think more clearly about how you receive value from the healthcare supply chain.

Before discussing each of the major elements, I'd like to clarify the meaning of the word *providers,* a commonly used term in the healthcare industry. Many doctors do not like to be called providers, and that's understandable, given their minimum of six years of postgraduate education and training. However, as they relate to the supply chain, doctors represent one type of provider. Other types of providers can include behavioral health professionals, nurses and nurse practitioners, dentists, social workers, and alternative and integrated medicine practitioners; any of these providers may work alone, in a small practice, or in an institution (such as a hospital or a nursing home). In simple terms, providers are suppliers of professional services to the system, and consumers are users of their services. The previous figure shows the main types of suppliers and the main generators of demand in an organized system of healthcare. Let's look closely at the elements of the healthcare supply chain, beginning with the supply side in the next figure:

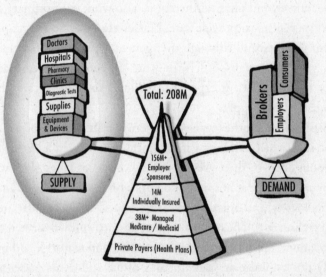

Doctors are the most obvious providers because they are the people with whom you have the most contact when you need care. Their role in the supply chain is to provide hands-on medical care and health information to patients. They also order diagnostic tests and procedures they deem necessary in order to evaluate a patient's condition. Primary care doctors in internal medicine, family practice, pediatrics, and, increasingly, obstetrics-gynecology (OB-GYN) and gerontology manage the overall health of their patients and evaluate whether patients need to see a specialist or take medication to control a particular condition. As we'll discuss further in chapter

8, many types of specialty physicians are increasingly assuming the role of primary care physician under a model known as the patient-centered medical home. Primary care doctors often are aided by physician assistants or nurse practitioners, who are also highly trained and help manage the patient load. Specialists such as orthopedists, neurologists, oncologists, and podiatrists have additional medical training focusing on a specific part of the anatomy, a particular illness, or a certain population group. Doctors can practice alone, in groups with similar types of doctors, or in multispecialty clinics where primary care doctors and specialists work side by side. Other licensed healthcare professionals, including physician assistants, nurse practitioners, nurses, and physical therapists, also work with primary care doctors and specialists to provide care. Nurses are essential to the process of caring for patients, and although they generally prepare patients for exams and carry out physicians' orders, they are the human thread that stitches together the total patient experience. Much like primary care physicians, nurses are in short supply.

Hospitals are another type of care provider that offers specialized facilities and infrastructure along with medical expertise. In addition to emergency room doctors, there are physicians, known as *hospitalists*, who practice primarily on-site at hospitals; doctors who specialize in certain diseases (e.g., oncologists) and organs (e.g., cardiologists); and, of course, nurses and medical technicians. The medical staff at hospitals provides emergency, surgical, inpatient, outpatient (sometimes called ambulatory), and other care typically not available at your doctor's office and treats patients in very serious situations for which a primary care doctor might not have the necessary expertise, equipment, or environment (such as an operating room). Most people don't realize that the majority of doctors in hospitals (besides ER doctors and hospitalists) are not there all the time. When they are not in the hospital, they run practices, admit patients, perform procedures and do "rounds" where they check in on their patients. Many hospitals have specialized units or *centers of excellence* staffed by highly trained specialists who perform complex procedures such as heart or lung transplants, hip or knee replacements, or cancer treatments. Other hospitals may specialize in treating burn victims or spinal injuries. Still others are known as *skilled* *nursing facilities* (or *post-acute facilities*) where patients may complete their recovery. Hospitals, whether general or dedicated to a particular specialty, provide concentrated expertise combined with the equipment, supplies, and environment necessary to treat serious illnesses and conditions. Quite often, general hospitals in highly populated areas also have clinics distributed around the flagship hospital to extend the hospital's expertise into the communities they serve. These clinics usually perform only outpatient procedures and tests.

Diagnostic centers are another type of care provider that most healthcare consumers encounter. These include medical labs, imaging centers (where you receive X-rays, magnetic resonance imaging [MRI], and other advanced types of radiological imaging), and a variety of centers that specialize in such things as cardiac, pulmonary, and gastroenterological (digestive tract) testing. Although the results from these tests may be reviewed by highly specialized physicians (e.g., radiologists) and technicians, they typically are passed directly to the physician who ordered them.

Pharmacies fill prescriptions written by doctors and other authorized healthcare professionals and check to see whether the medication prescribed is covered by the patient's health plan so they can determine how much money the consumer owes and how much to bill to the health plan. They also add value by alerting patients to possible drug interactions and explaining exactly how and when to take various medications. Some pharmacists make recommendations of over-the-counter remedies for patients who don't feel sick enough to go to the doctor. In addition, pharmacy benefit managers— who work for the pharmacy, for various health plans, or independently— establish formularies, check whether patients are covered for certain medications, and determine when generic drugs may be substituted.

Clinics of various types provide services that are targeted to consumer needs. Examples include urgent care clinics for non-life-threatening emergencies; walk-in clinics for people who may be from a different town, may not have a regular primary care doctor, or may need to access care during hours that extend beyond their doctor's office hours; and specialized clinics, such as those that deal exclusively with women's health issues. Retail clinics, part of a growing trend to improve convenience, have begun to spring up in large discount retail stores that also have in-house pharmacies. These clinics are usually staffed by nurses or nurse practitioners who are able to provide services such as flu vaccinations and common diagnostic tests (such as checking for strep throat). If antibiotics are prescribed, patients can have them filled on site.

Vendors of medical equipment, devices, and supplies sell or rent items such as oxygen transport systems, glucose meters, blood pressure cuffs, crutches, canes, back braces, wheelchairs, home intravenous drug infusion systems, and other tangible items used directly by healthcare consumers. Items that can be reused by multiple patients are often referred to as *durable medical equipment*. There are also disposable supplies for eye care, wound care, incontinence management, ostomy management, and many other medical conditions. These supplies are usually expensive and may not be available in your corner drugstore, but they are used and disposed of on a regular basis by many healthcare consumers. Some device and equipment manufacturers sell only to hospitals, doctors, clinics and diagnostic centers—an important fact to keep in mind as we look at how the parts of the healthcare system work together. They sell single-use items such as drug-eluting stents and pacemakers as well as imaging machines, dialysis machines, electronic patient monitoring stations, and other expensive capital items that a consumer, unless endowed with a fortune, would not typically purchase for personal use. Also, as I mentioned earlier, pharmaceutical companies (which develop drugs) and other biotechnology entities supply an array of goods in bulk to pharmacies and hospitals (as well as samples to doctors). The process of developing these applied technologies is costly, and the high price of these products often reflects the manufacturer's need to recoup development costs. Not all equipment and supply companies provide the same level of quality or charge the same amount for their goods. Because the typical consumer lacks expertise in this area, it is the job of the organizer of the supply chain to select companies and products that offer high quality at the best price.

As shown in the following figure, there are also several elements on the demand side of the healthcare supply chain:

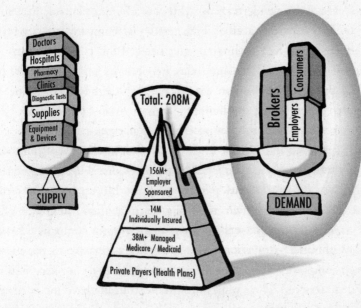

Employers, as they relate to the healthcare supply chain, are aggregators of healthcare consumers. In other words, they provide an entry point for consumers into the healthcare supply chain through financial arrangements they make with the health plans they offer to employees. Many people may not realize the value added by employers, who often pay a large percentage of the total healthcare premium cost for their employees. For the most part, whether or not an employer offers health benefits depends on its size and financial status. For example, some small employers offer only very basic coverage with high out-of-pocket costs for their employees, or they do not offer health insurance at all. On the other hand, many larger employers go beyond basic health insurance to offer wellness and disease management programs that help employees stay healthy and manage chronic illnesses such as diabetes. The role of the employer will be discussed in the next chapter, but it should be understood that since the mid-twentieth century, it has been almost a given that employers in the United States are directly involved in the healthcare supply chain to make sure their employees have access to health insurance coverage. In many other countries, this is absolutely not the case.

Brokers are independent agents who play an important role in helping consumers and employers decide which health plan company and what types of benefits will best meet their respective needs. Brokers help organize the demand side of the supply chain. Today, between 75 percent and 100 percent[2] of all private health insurance is purchased through more than one million licensed life and health insurance brokers across the United States.[3] Brokers are perceived as advocates for purchasers of all types including senior citizens, self-employed individuals, small and mid-sized employer groups, and large, multistate employers. Brokers who primarily distribute group benefits typically have a direct relationship with employers. Most people who receive insurance benefits through their employers (i.e., more than 150 million of us) do not know that brokers are the primary drivers of our companies' benefit choices. Within the past few years, rising healthcare costs and increased benefit design complexity have created more opportunities for brokers to differentiate their services. Their responsibilities historically have included purchasing guidance, enrollment assistance, billing and claims status inquiries, and policy renewals, though some brokers now include administration of wellness and other preventive health programs in their spectra of services. The role of brokers will change as a result of healthcare reform laws that call for the creation of online health insurance "exchanges" in each state. These exchanges will allow consumers to select insurance coverage themselves and enroll directly in a health plan. (See chapters 5 and 8 for more details.) The changing role of brokers is similar to how travel agents have had to adapt ever since online travel sites have enabled consumers to book their own flights and hotels. The travel agencies that still exist today have found ways to add significant value for their customers by offering trip insights and experiences that go beyond information found online.

Consumers, people like you and me, generate the demand on the demand side of the supply chain. The challenge is that we are not all alike. We require different amounts and types of healthcare depending on our age, life stage, health status, financial situation, and values (which include factors such as our religious upbringings, cultural backgrounds, and personal philosophies). The following figure, the healthcare life stage graph, shows that our need for healthcare generally follows a predictable but unsettling pattern as we move from birth to death. Because our health status usually peaks in our prime and declines with age, and our income typically peaks during middle age and then declines, our demand for healthcare services begins to grow substantially at the same time as our income is declining. This affordability challenge is made worse by the fact that we are living longer than ever before. Moreover, as the graph shows, one single event such as an accident or an acute illness can instantly change a person's health status and income, creating difficult challenges at unpredictable times.

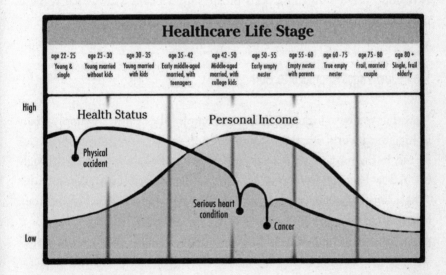

Who Manages the Supply Chain?

In the middle of the supply chain are **payers**, commonly known as **health plans**, organizing systems of benefits and care to balance supply and demand within an economic set of constraints (i.e., at an affordable price). As the previous supply chain illustration shows, private payers—known to most consumers as insurance companies such as Blue Cross Blue Shield affiliates, Aetna, CIGNA, United Health Group, and Humana—carry out this function. Public payers such as the federal and state governments oversee Medicare, Medicaid, and several other programs, but as we will see, they do not typically organize benefits and care in the same manner as private plans.

There are also many other elements of the supply chain that are a step or more removed from the consumer, such as pharmaceutical companies that sell supplies to pharmacies, as well as research organizations that break new ground regarding medical science and applied technologies. In addition, there are many federal and state regulatory bodies that have an impact on virtually every element of the supply chain. In order to stay on point, I have concentrated on those parts of the supply chain with which you are most likely to come into direct contact as a healthcare consumer.

The Yellow Pages Approach to Getting Care

Now that you have seen how large and complex the healthcare supply chain is, imagine a world where it's completely up to you to organize all the elements. In the most extreme cases, you might find yourself flipping through the Yellow Pages or surfing the Internet to find a doctor. If you look under "Physicians," there is a very lengthy list. Where would you start? If your foot hurt, would you go to an orthopedist, an internist, a nephrologist, or a podiatrist? Assuming you were able to direct yourself to the correct specialty, how would you know which doctor to choose? Would you select a doctor based on cost, on whether someone you know has seen her, or on where she went to medical school? Adding to your confusion would be the fact that you have no idea what services you need, so you could not possibly know how much your appointment would cost. In short, you would be stuck in the middle of a very complex nonsystem with no information on quality or cost and no one to help you down the path that makes the most sense for you. Could you organize your own supply chain of doctors, hospitals (in the event you need surgery for your foot), pharmacies, diagnostic testing services, and medical supplies that would ensure that you'd receive high-quality care at a predetermined price? Or would you truly be in the heart of the healthcare jungle?

Balancing Supply and Demand: Organizers of the Supply Chain

In order for any supply chain to exist, someone has to develop business arrangements with suppliers or vendors who meet a set of quality, cost, and service standards. In the case of Lexus brand automobiles, the supply chain is organized by Toyota®, which negotiates contracts with certain vendors that have met its requirements. These contracts and the complex negotiations that precede them are invisible to you if you purchase a Lexus, but they are a critical part of its creation. Similarly, you do not see the technology that enables service information to be accessed by all Lexus service departments; however, without it, you would not receive the comprehensive, coordinated service you have come to expect.

In healthcare, the organizers of the supply chain are private payers (health plans) as well as the federal government and individual state governments in the role of public payers. These entities bring together certain providers and vendors into a network that can give you healthcare at a price within your means and that is accessible to you either directly (through an individual or "self-pay" plan) or through your employer.

The 2010 census revealed that there are approximately 310 million Americans.[4] Estimates of the number of uninsured range from twenty-five million to just over fifty million people.[5] Even if you take the high end of that range, that means more than 250 million Americans are covered by health insurance and, therefore, receive care in the context of at least a partially organized healthcare supply chain. One of the goals of the healthcare reform law is to create an opportunity for a significant percentage of the uninsured to become part of the organized healthcare supply chain through access to health insurance coverage.

Now, let's take a look at who organizes the healthcare supply chain for those 250 million Americans.

Private payers, such as health plans, provide medical and specialty coverage for more than 200 million people in the United States.[6] Approximately seven hundred private payers[7] negotiate competitive pricing arrangements with doctors, hospitals, diagnostic companies, pharmacy benefit managers, and vendors of supplies and equipment and then bundle this vast array of complex services into benefit plans that meet the needs of employers and individuals. Private payers sell their benefit plans to whomever is in charge of benefits (often the human resource department) at the employer as well as to people seeking coverage on their own (either directly or through a broker), enabling consumers to enroll in the plans and access the doctors, hospitals, and care facilities that compose their "delivery network." Private payers also make this coverage available for a period of time (through the COBRA program) to people who had been covered under their employer's health coverage but who no longer receive health benefits through an employer group. Private payers provide service to consumers, providers, pharmacists, employers, and brokers by answering questions about which services are covered for consumers in their benefit plans. In addition, private payers manage contracts and relationships with all parts of the supply chain, keep track of premium payments made by employers or individuals, process claims based on negotiated prices, and determine who is responsible for paying which portion of the costs.

Historically, private payers have played a transaction-oriented role in the supply chain, processing claims that come in and authorizing payment for covered services. Depending upon the type of benefit plan, payers also get involved to various degrees in driving efficient use of healthcare resources, ensuring consumers are getting appropriate care from appropriate providers, and proactively helping consumers pursue better health and wellness. (Note: Payers that take on financial risk are also regarded as "health insurers," whereas payers that organize the system of benefits and care and then process transactions for self-funded employer groups are called third-party administrators [TPAs] or administrative-services-only providers [ASOs]. Health plans typically offer employers a choice of insured or self-funded products and are capable of administering both.)

Public payers, such as federal and state governments, also organize supply chains for health coverage for about 110 million people in the United States, approximately one-third of whom choose to assign their benefit coverage to private health plans through such programs as Medicare Advantage and managed Medicaid. The government establishes benefit packages for various segments of our society for whom it is responsible by law, determines who will be eligible for these benefits, negotiates pricing arrangements with certain providers and hospitals, and manages (or contracts with a private payer to manage) the claims payments and other financial operations. See the benefits plan chart that follows for more detail on health coverage plans organized by the state and federal governments.

Major Government-Organized Health Benefit Plans

Product	Whom It Is For	Supply Chain Organizer	Approximate Number of Beneficiaries
Medicare	• people age 65 and over • people under age 65 with certain disabilities • people of all ages with end-stage renal disease	federal government via the Centers for Medicare and Medicaid Services (CMS)	46.6 million[8]
Medicaid	primarily for people with very low income levels	state governments, with assistance and oversight from CMS	48.6 million[9]
TRICARE	active-duty military personnel and their families	federal government (Department of Defense)	9.6 million[10]
Department of Veterans Affairs	honorably discharged veterans and their dependents	federal government (Department of Veterans Affairs)	8.0 million[11]
Federal Employee Health Benefits Program	employees of the federal government and their families	federal government, which in most cases contracts with private payers to supply the benefits administration	8.0 million[12]

Understanding the Cost and Value of Healthcare

Everywhere you turn, you hear that the US healthcare system (the supply chain of healthcare) delivers too little quality for too much cost. While this is generally true, it is also true that the roughly 250 million insured Americans who are part of the healthcare supply chain do not all receive healthcare products of equivalent value—just as the car models they drive have different features, quality, and pricing. These days, policy makers spend a significant amount of energy trying to identify the best aspects of the private and public payers' respective supply chain models and combine them to deliver high healthcare value to all Americans.

But what does value in healthcare really mean? Let's start with an explanation of how we calculate the total cost of healthcare, and then we will look at how to determine the value we are getting from the money we spend. The total cost of healthcare for either an individual or a population of patients equals the price that is paid for each unit of care received (such as an office visit, a prescription, or a hospital stay) multiplied by the number of occurrences of each of those units.

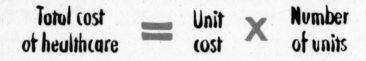

$$\text{Total cost of healthcare} = \text{Unit cost} \times \text{Number of units}$$

In order to deliver healthcare for fewer dollars, we need to systematically manage both the unit cost and the number of units. You've already seen that in a supply chain, unit prices are prenegotiated, but the number of units is more variable because it is based on demand. Therefore, if we can lower the number of units "produced," then you would expect that we would be able to spend less money on healthcare. The challenge is how to determine who should get which units (procedures, pharmaceuticals, and other therapies). Clearly, doctors largely control the ability to order units of healthcare treatments, tests, and prescriptions because they are the ones licensed to practice medicine. But as we have seen, there is great variation in the way doctors treat patients who have the same condition. The ideal way to produce higher-quality healthcare is to ensure that doctors order and deliver the types of units that will produce the best outcomes (the best health status results) for their patients. The equation shown in the following figure may clarify the definition of healthcare value:

$$\text{Healthcare value} = \frac{\text{Health status (outcomes)}}{\text{Total cost of healthcare}}$$

In this value equation, we take the total cost of healthcare from the previous equation and bring in the important concept of outcomes produced by the units of care. If we can produce better outcomes (such as an asthmatic child staying out of the emergency room) for a lower total cost (by prescribing and monitoring the child's use of a relatively inexpensive preventive asthma inhaler, for example), then the value this patient receives is greater than if she had to be treated, perhaps repeatedly, in the emergency room where the cost would have been higher. The *effectiveness* or *outcome* of the results produced by the units determines the level of value we are getting for the money we spend on healthcare. Our ultimate goal is to increase the value we get for every healthcare dollar we spend.

How do we achieve this ambitious goal? This is a question that challenges our healthcare system (and I will offer a solution in chapter 8). But much work has already been done in pursuit of higher value and quality, and it is useful to understand the approaches that currently exist. In the United States, two models organized around providers have emerged: the *organized system of payment* and the *integrated delivery system*. In addition, health plans are exploring the model of *organized systems of benefits and care* (also known as *managed care*). Let's take a look at each of these models.

Organized Systems of Payment

Historically, the government has tried to address this question, in large part by focusing on managing unit cost. For example, the government-organized supply chains for Medicare and state Medicaid programs essentially have been organized systems of payment. This means that while the government establishes (or imposes) pricing with its providers and suppliers regarding reimbursement for care delivery, the care itself is not systematically organized or coordinated in any substantial way. In most cases, the primary care doctors, specialists, imaging centers, pharmacies, hospitals, and other parts of the supply chain are not formally affiliated with one another in terms of the sharing of information systems or the coordination of referrals and care; their only connection with one another is that they all have pricing contracts with the government. With a few notable exceptions (which I will describe later in this chapter), our government primarily serves as an organizer of payments, not an organizer of both payments and care.

Integrated Delivery Systems

While our government has focused largely on the cost component of our healthcare system's inefficiency, providers have tried to improve the way care is coordinated and delivered—by assembling integrated delivery systems. Under this care delivery model, one or more hospitals along with physicians, diagnostic centers, and other components of the supply side of the supply chain strive to share information, minimize duplication, and make treatment decisions based upon the institutional best practices for the patient's given situation. In the private sector, integrated delivery systems typically are organized in urban or high-density suburban areas containing one or more leading hospitals. Nearby private physician practices, and often physicians with academic relationships to local universities, set up localized delivery systems that include hospitals, specialists, and primary care doctors. Doctors are increasingly moving toward being employed by or having their practices owned by the same entity that owns the hospitals in these integrated delivery systems.[13] Although these entities might not all be located in the same building, they work with one another in a systematic, coordinated way, giving patients the impression of having all services under one roof. Within integrated delivery networks, providers can often coordinate units of care better because they can access health information about a particular patient from other providers who may also have cared for the patient. For example, because the providers all share the same information systems, it is unlikely that two different doctors would order duplicate X-rays for your injured ankle.

However, although your care may be well *coordinated* in these settings, from a systems view, the *value* of the care is questioned by some. Why is this? In order to make full use of expensive equipment and hospital beds that might otherwise sit empty at times, there is often pressure to order more care than meets the guidelines for best practices. For example, when I was an executive with an integrated delivery system that owned hospitals, physician groups, pharmacies, and diagnostic centers, there was always a lot of pressure to keep the beds filled and the equipment humming because of the misguided notion that fully utilizing the beds and equipment would lead to greater efficiency. Such logic might succeed in generating revenue to pay for the capital investments made by the hospital or imaging center that bought the medical equipment; however, it unnecessarily drives up the number of units—the second variable in the Total Cost of Healthcare equation—making our healthcare system as a whole less cost-effective and more expensive. The problem with most "health systems" (the name often given to integrated delivery systems) is that in most cases, the coordination of care is not managed by the same entity that manages the payment of the care, so there is little incentive to deliver care in the most cost-effective way. In other words, the integrated delivery system is just operating on the supply side of the supply chain.

To attempt to address this issue, healthcare reform legislation calls for the creation of Accountable Care Organizations (ACOs) for the care of Medicare recipients. While ACOs are still at an early point in their evolution, they are intended to be healthcare entities consisting of affiliated providers who take responsibility for coordinating and delivering a complete continuum of care to their patient populations in a high-quality and efficient manner. The main point about early ACO legislation is that the government will share savings with hospitals and doctors who order units of services and price these services appropriately (i.e., are more cost-effective) while achieving improved outcomes. ACOs will likely evolve into risk-bearing entities responsible for providing care for a population of patients within a fixed budget; ACOs will thereby have the potential to realize both financial upside and financial downside based on how effectively they manage patient care. Similarly, the legislation encourages the formation of a professional practice model called the patient-centered medical home in which doctors are accountable for coordinating all the care their patients need, whether it be specialty care, hospitalization, physical therapy, or other covered services. (See chapter 8 for more details.)

Organized Systems of Payments and Care: A Step in the Right Direction

Now let's look at an example of a government-organized payment and care delivery system in which the same party providing the care also pays for it: the Department of Veterans Affairs (the VA), which offers military personnel care through an integrated system of government-owned (and privately subcontracted) hospitals and clinics, along with dedicated health professionals. There is a certain elegant simplicity to the electronic sharing of information (i.e., electronic health records) about VA beneficiaries (veterans who are patients), which is made possible because these patients receive the majority of their care at VA facilities that all run on common systems, and patients stay in the system for their entire lives (in contrast to most US citizens, who change health plans multiple times). The VA is a glimpse of what a single-payer system looks like, where the payments and care are under centralized control.

From a systems science perspective, an important point here is that both the VA (for retired military) and TRICARE (the health program for active military) follow the pattern of centralized control for the US defense system: funding through taxation (not through private insurance premiums). This funding arrangement, run by the government in this case, disconnects employers and consumers from the real cost of care, which gives them little incentive to make decisions that would control costs to drive more healthcare value.

In the private sector, there are examples similar to the VA where there is a benefit plan that lines up directly with an integrated delivery system, but where the care provided is not paid for by taxes. One of the better-known is Kaiser Permanente®, where primary care, specialty care, diagnostic testing, and even pharmacies are located at company-run health centers and paid for by Kaiser Health Plans. Kaiser has a good understanding of how to apply information technology in its integrated delivery system to improve healthcare value for its patients and has invested billions of dollars in enterprise information systems to coordinate patient scheduling and treatments and maintain electronic records. Here, too, consumers and employers are not completely connected to the actual cost of healthcare, but because they must pay insurance premiums and some level of co-payments, they have at least a basic approximation of their annual costs.

However, comprehensive integrated delivery systems where the benefit plan is also coordinated by the same organization, like Kaiser and the VA, are all too rare in both the public and private sectors. This is because they require patient populations large enough to create sufficient scale; tremendous amounts of financial capital for facilities, equipment, information systems, and salaries; and medical professionals who are willing to work as employees. Because these examples of comprehensive integrated delivery systems are generally in physical campus settings that are relatively easy for policy makers to visit and understand, sometimes policy makers lose sight of the fact that in most of the United States, circumstances make it difficult to create and sustain similar integrated delivery systems.

In the majority of large American cities, and certainly in suburban and rural settings, the delivery of care to you as a consumer is more typically fragmented due to a combination of factors, including provider competition (multiple hospitals, independent physicians, different pharmacy chains, etc.) and consumer desire for choice. An example of this fragmented care is that a painkiller prescribed by a specialist may never make it into the medical records kept by the primary care doctor who saw you initially for the same illness or injury. Similarly, test results are not systematically sent from one doctor to another, often resulting in repetition of the same test by multiple physicians. Even referrals from primary care doctors to specialists are based largely on which specialist a given primary care doctor knows—not on an objective assessment of who would be the best specialist to perform a particular procedure or even who has the most competitive pricing. Without an organized delivery system that is tied into a benefit plan, there is no systematic way to predict costs, encourage high-quality delivery of care, or minimize overlap. As a result, it is up to the individual patient or doctor to push through the healthcare jungle and try to create order out of the chaos. When care and payments are truly coordinated, it's almost accidental. Wouldn't it be better to make it systematic?

Organized Payment and Integrated Delivery Are Good but Can Be Made Better

My point, and a major point of this book, is that neither an organized system of payment nor an integrated delivery system approach alone can optimally serve the whole US population. By taking the best aspects of integrated delivery systems and organized systems of payment and care, we can develop a healthcare system that works for most Americans—whether they live in a big city, a suburb, or a rural setting. Before we discuss this, though, let's examine a couple of systematic examples from other industries to lay the groundwork for what we can accomplish in healthcare.

The Supply Chains of Big-Box Retail Stores and Their Virtual Cousins

In order to better understand the value of a fully functioning supply chain, let's take a trip to our local Walmart. Walmart takes a set of demands from its customers, such as the need for reasonably priced hygiene items or photography products and services, and organizes a set of suppliers and service providers to meet these needs. Walmart also carefully manages this supply chain and makes adjustments as it learns more about its customers' needs and preferences. For example, Walmart may know that around the holidays, consumers buy more digital memory chips for their digital cameras, so Walmart works with its suppliers to ensure adequate inventory at those peak times. It also monitors demand for certain items on a real-time basis. If it sees demand increase for a particular item—for example, a certain type of nutrition bar that consumers are snapping up because of a successful advertising campaign—it orders more of that item from its supplier. And if Walmart notices certain products being returned over and over, Walmart either discusses the problem with its supplier or stops carrying these items. Walmart continually and systematically monitors its inventory, the performance of its suppliers, and the demands of its consumers in order to make sure the supply meets the consumers' demand for the highest-quality products at the lowest prices. These systematic principles of effective price negotiation, efficient distribution, constant monitoring of customer preferences, and strict attention to quality enable Walmart to succeed both when the overall economy is stable and during periods of economic challenge.

Online retailer Amazon is an example of another well-designed system of logistics and supply-chain management that is virtual (i.e., nonphysical). Although you can't walk the aisles of an Amazon store, its offers and prices are clearly communicated to the prospective purchaser in an online encounter. Importantly, consumers have a sense of exactly what they are getting for a certain price and when it will arrive. In addition, consumers can view the product and read reviews from others who have previously experienced it. This example exists in stark contrast to the current state of healthcare purchasing, where consumers stand mired in the jungle without a clear sense of what is being delivered, what that delivery will cost, and what its ultimate value is. As with Walmart, the Amazon experience did not evolve randomly as a result of multiple suppliers interacting under their traditional models, but rather was designed and engineered by Amazon (using the best of conventional physical supply-chain management) with the virtual consumer in mind.

The approach of Amazon has been telling. Consumers have signaled their strong approval of the Amazon model, continuously increasing their online buying at the expense of traditional stores that you can physically enter and whose merchandise you can touch before buying. Amazon also pioneered reliable delivery in electronic form of products that used to be exclusively in physical form (e.g., book delivery via an electronic reading device). The success of this innovation continues even amid recent economic uncertainty, showing that when consumers are exposed to a clearly communicated value proposition that delivers value to them in a more convenient way, they tend to embrace it.

So what does Walmart or Amazon have to do with the US healthcare system? Obviously, healthcare is much more complex than a big-box chain store. After all, retail stores primarily provide products you can touch, feel, or see, while healthcare is focused on a very specialized set of services. However, just as we explored the successes of the manufacturer of the Lexus in chapter 3, there is much we can learn from the systematic way in which stores like Walmart organize and manage their supply chains. Every Walmart store throughout the country has an organized supply chain with prenegotiated pricing. In addition, the pricing is clearly communicated and payment is understood and collected at the moment you go through checkout (at the point of service). In other words, the pricing is visible and transparent to everyone from the consumer to the company's chief financial officer to the cashier ringing up the sale. Amazon's online checkout process is just as transparent.

Healthcare Lacks Pricing Transparency for Consumers and Providers

In contrast to retail, pricing in healthcare is rarely fully understood by the consumer or doctor's office. Although in many cases the healthcare supply chain organizers have negotiated pricing and discounts with providers and suppliers, that pricing is not transparent or clearly communicated to patients and providers. If it were, we would know exactly how much of our health insurance premium is used to pay for medical expenses we actually incur versus how much is used to protect us from spending all of our savings should a medical catastrophe occur (the insurance portion of our premium). We would also know the actual cost of a three-month supply of our cholesterol medication—not just the forty dollars or sixty dollars we are required to pay when we pick up the prescription. Instead, we simply pay what we are asked to pay and assume we'll be covered for whatever we need. And rarely do we know in advance of a procedure or an appointment the real cost of these services. This approach would never work in retail, and it is one of the reasons our healthcare system is in such dire financial straits. As I mentioned before, with an absence of pricing information, it is difficult (if not impossible) for a consumer to determine value. And if consumers do not make healthcare choices based on value (whether we are getting high-quality care at a reasonable price), then we will simply continue to pay what we are told to pay, and we will have no reason to drive our healthcare system to become more cost-effective. As we saw in chapter 3, this is exactly what happened to buyers of high-end cars before Japanese automakers in the 1980s showed the world that a better car could be produced for less money. If automobile pricing had not been transparent in the 1980s, it would have been difficult, if not impossible, for Japanese automakers to enter the marketplace and competitively force the issue of producing a higher-quality product at a lower cost.

In addition to the pricing differences between retail chains and the healthcare delivery system, there is another important difference between retail and healthcare. Retail stores like Walmart offer all their products under one roof—or in the case of online stores like Amazon, on one site. This one-stop shopping approach enables the consumer to buy many different items, from beverages and candy to tablecloths and candles, all at the same place. In contrast, the healthcare delivery system is most often spread over a number of different physical locations. For example, if you go to your primary care doctor for a checkup, you will often need to make a separate stop at a lab for blood work. Similarly, if you have a knee problem, you might go from your primary care doctor to a specialist's office and sometimes to a separate location for diagnostic tests. If you need to see the physical therapist or need to have surgery, you probably have to make additional trips. Each of these stops creates additional complexity for consumers and providers alike. The physical separation of many providers from one another is even more reason for our healthcare system to apply the fundamental supply-chain management principles of the retail world in order to develop a more seamless, coordinated system. It may seem disrespectful to regard physicians, who are highly educated and make life-and-death decisions, as suppliers to be organized in a supply chain. But from a systems science perspective, that is the case. There are numerous other examples of life-and-death suppliers in other supply chains, from the seemingly simple engineering and manufacturing of a seat belt to the complex construction of bridges and jet airliners.

Private Payers' Attempts to Systematize Healthcare

Over the past several decades, healthcare experts in the United States have experimented with various ways to rein in costs and improve the quality of our healthcare supply chain in a systematic way. We started with basic health insurance in the 1950s, when experienced insurance risk management professionals (called *actuaries*) tried to predict, based on past experience with similar groups of people, how much care would be used for a given population. The actuaries then set a price for the insurance premium based on how much care they thought this group of people would receive over a set period of time, usually one year. During some years, people used more care than predicted, and in other years, they used less. The challenge for the insurance company was to accurately predict how much care a given population would consume in one year (the "demand") and to set a price for insurance premiums that would cover the total cost of care. Despite the best efforts of these insurance companies, their approach often missed the mark because it largely relied on trying to predict the care that would be used, rather than on organizing and managing the cost, volume, and quality of services provided.

In the 1980s, the concept of managed care began to evolve. As its name suggests, managed care marked the beginning of a more systematic approach to healthcare, where instead of predicting or guessing how much care people would use, health maintenance organizations (HMOs) set up organized networks of doctors, hospitals, pharmacies, and vendors of equipment and medical supplies. Pricing was negotiated in advance with each of the elements of what became the healthcare supply chain. The "maintenance" in "health maintenance organization" was similar to the Lexus service approach in chapter 3: if you have preventive checkups and screenings at regular intervals and according to established guidelines, then you may be more likely to stay healthy and less likely to need a big repair. HMOs introduced the primary care doctor as one who would take care of you as a whole person, not just as a broken ankle or a case of pneumonia. Through routine screenings, patient education, smoking cessation programs, parenting programs, and other initiatives considered innovative at the time, your HMO would not only treat you when you were sick, but also try to help you stay well. Best of all, your primary care doctor could help you find the right in-network specialist to treat the pain in your foot so you would not be stuck leafing through the phone book for a doctor or trying to build your own supply chain. Going from health insurance to health maintenance meant shifting from a reactive mode to one with more deliberate control over care and costs.

If healthcare was heading in a more systematic direction, then why did this fine nation not embrace the HMO model as its official system? The simple answer is that most Americans were not ready to acknowledge that in order to better manage care and costs, HMOs would have to establish guidelines for when patients should receive certain types of care as well as determine from whom they may receive it. So in addition to their roles as healers and promoters of health, primary care doctors were asked to determine when it was medically necessary for patients to see specialists, undergo tests, or get access to complex or even experimental treatments. Let's use a couple of examples to make this concept of medical necessity clear. If a patient were to see a doctor for a mole on her back, the doctor would typically remove it if it met the guidelines for removal; however, if it did not appear to be dangerous, then the doctor would ask the patient to return at regular intervals to have the growth checked. The patient could always choose to have the growth removed, but if removal was not judged by the primary care doctor to be medically necessary, then the patient would have to pay out of pocket for the care associated with removing the mole.

Another example of managed care guidelines has to do with the concept of self-referral to specialists. Let's go back to the example in chapter 2 of a hurt elbow from a tennis game. If you started your journey by going directly to the office of an orthopedic surgeon, the likelihood of having an imaging test or a minimally invasive surgical procedure known as arthroscopy would increase because the orthopedic specialist is trained to diagnose and treat in a particular way. While the orthopedist is trying in earnest to solve the patient's problem, both test and procedure are expensive, and the procedure risks complications. Under the health maintenance model, the patient would have been seen by a primary care physician who would have discussed the possible next steps, including self-care options (such as rest, ice, compression, and elevation) and less invasive professional treatments (such as physical therapy). This approach has the potential to reduce the number of unnecessary tests and surgical procedures while still providing the patient with a positive outcome.

In conventional managed care, there are also examples where testing or procedures that do, in fact, make good medical sense are denied or the barriers to obtaining them are too high. This type of situation typically occurs in specialty areas such as cancer treatment. For example, an oncologist may know about new therapies or specialty drug combinations that are producing improved health outcomes, but the people who set guidelines in managed care organizations might not yet know about these therapies or drugs. It's rare that such therapies don't ultimately get approved, but when there is a lag between the testing of new treatments and their approval by managed care organizations, it is frustrating for both the oncologist and the patient. Overall, however, some friction in the system is good because not all treatments physicians want to pursue are evidence based, nor are all less invasive approaches necessarily the right treatment for every patient. The public relations challenge for managed care organizations such as HMOs and for our healthcare system in general is to control costs, improve quality, and help consumers understand that in order to accomplish both of these goals in an organized system of benefits and care, we need to rely on rules, limits, and informed decisions regarding value and effectiveness. Healthcare reform legislation calls for the creation of patient-centered medical homes (PCMHs), a care delivery model in which a doctor or group of doctors organizes both primary and specialty care for patients. Although the name has changed, the PCMH model has distinct similarities to the primary care "gatekeeper" in conventional managed care. This is an example of our government constructively considering useful models from private health plans.

Health Plans Have Broad Perspective to Lead Change

The United States is at a critical juncture for healthcare. As more people live longer and our population increases, our overall health status as a nation is declining, and the total demand for healthcare services will continue to rise. Put simply, more people are in need of more care, which means more money will be spent on healthcare unless we find a systematic way to provide this care more cost-effectively while also helping people become as healthy as possible. There are ongoing policy debates in Washington, DC, about how much money should be raised and how it should be distributed, from a payment perspective, across the healthcare supply chain. However, agreeing on an exact dollar amount to be allotted for each component in healthcare is far less important than designing our system to provide high-quality care consistently and more cost-effectively than it does today. We need to figure out how to do more for less under any circumstance. So, who has a broad view of all the elements of the healthcare system and is in the best position to lead this effort? I contend that private health plans, like the ones running today's managed care programs, are best positioned (despite current shortcomings) to show leadership in systematically engineering the US healthcare system because they already sit at the center of the healthcare supply chain. In this capacity, they manage large groups of people, and they have sophisticated information technology that can be used as the starting point for improving our healthcare system.

To give you some perspective on the scale of these private enterprises, the biggest private payers in the United States manage larger populations than the populations of entire countries such as the Netherlands, Sweden, and even Canada, to which our own healthcare system is compared. Private payers negotiate contracts and pull together doctors, hospitals, pharmacies, retail clinics, diagnostic laboratories, and equipment and device suppliers to form a supply chain (and all of these elements must meet certain standards for quality and agree to adhere to guidelines in order to be paid). In this role of supply chain organizer, private payers are at the heart of interactions with all the supply chain elements. Like the wise man in the parable in chapter 2, private payers already touch all the parts of the system and are in the best position to see the system as a whole. Consequently, health plans understand that when it comes to effectively managing the supply side of the supply chain, organized systems of payment alone are insufficient. Health plans also realize that while integrated delivery system models can be very effective where available, in many geographic areas, we need to create virtual supply chains with otherwise disconnected elements in order to create an organized system of care for consumers.

So how do we take advantage of this system knowledge to create substantially higher value in the healthcare supply chain? As I mentioned in chapter 1, in order to solve complex problems such as healthcare, it is important to focus our energy on the variables that matter most. A common cliché in healthcare is that the doctor's pen (or perhaps a computer keyboard) is the most powerful force in healthcare. There is no doubt that the doctor and his pen may be the strongest, but it is not the *only* systems element that determines healthcare value. The design of the benefits plan for healthcare consumers is another powerful force that is influenced by several key stakeholders. (In the next chapter we'll learn more about these stakeholders.)

Now that you understand the healthcare supply chain, you are one step closer to seeing how we can improve the healthcare system. Once you learn about the key stakeholders in the system and about the way money and incentives work today (as you will in chapter 7), you will see the opportunity we have to dramatically improve value in the US healthcare system by thoughtfully designing benefits plans tailored to individuals. Tailored benefits plans (rather than today's one-size-fits-all approach), combined with cost-effective supply-chain management, can knock 20–30 percent off the total amount we are spending on healthcare, while improving the quality of health outcomes across our entire population.[14] Considering both benefits and care in this manner is fundamental to what I call Integrated Healthcare Management.

In order to fix a broken system, whether it is in manufacturing, mail delivery, or healthcare, one of the first steps is to look closely at the needs of the constituents or "players" in the system. In chapter 5, we will examine what consumers, providers, employers, and brokers need from the healthcare system and how those needs are changing.

Chapter 5

The Perspectives of Healthcare Constituents

What you see and hear depends a good deal on where you are standing.
—C. S. LEWIS, *THE MAGICIAN'S NEPHEW*, 1966

I n chapter 4, we saw that few truly integrated delivery systems exist in this country and that most care is fragmented, with little coordination among the parts of the system. And as we saw in chapter 2, some of the parts of the system do not even know the others exist, let alone understand how they work. Classic systems-design techniques suggest that we must consider the interplay of people, processes, and technology in order to properly understand and design systematic solutions. In the case of the healthcare system, the constituents—the primary types of people who participate in the healthcare supply chain—include the people who consume, provide, finance, distribute, and manage healthcare products and services.

Designing an integrated, coordinated healthcare system where all the parts interact smoothly and efficiently requires us to step into the shoes of each of the following types of healthcare constituents—the major stake holders in the healthcare system: consumers, providers, employers, brokers, and health plans. What are their respective roles, responsibilities, and incentives? How does the system need to work for them? Are they getting what they need? How does one constituent's needs affect the other constituents? The following figure summarizes the life cycle of these con-stituents and their respective experiences with the US healthcare system over the course of a typical year. The model below assumes that the con-sumer's selection of a health plan is arranged by her employer, as it is for the majority of Americans with health insurance—more than 150 million people.[1] As we work through the constituent life cycles, I will point out some of the differences for people who buy insurance directly or receive it from the government. Only by understanding these life cycles and the interactions constituents have with one another can we begin to design a healthcare system that works for everyone. Let's begin by looking at these interactions through the eyes of the consumer.

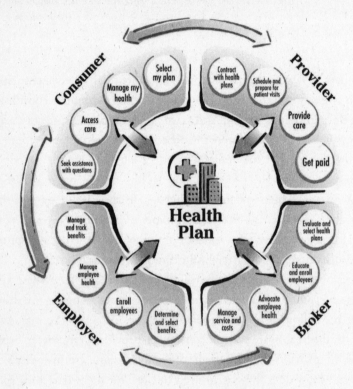

Consumers' Expanding Role in Healthcare Decision Making

As consumers, we are in the midst of an ever-changing healthcare jungle. Until recently, we paid little of the healthcare premium and enjoyed health benefits with low out-of-pocket costs. As a result, many of us have long thought of health benefits as an entitlement. But now, as healthcare infla-tion outstrips growth in the gross domestic product (GDP), employers are being forced to share more of the cost of healthcare coverage with their employees, reduce benefits, or eliminate coverage entirely. This afford-ability crisis is forcing many consumers to take greater responsibility for their healthcare decisions, including a larger stake in the financial implica-tions of their decisions. However, people don't necessarily want greater responsibility. I often say that consumers did not ask for consumer-directed healthcare; however, economic realities are driving change. And yet, for many families, the total amount paid for health insurance premiums, deductibles, and co-insurance ends up being one of their largest total house-hold expenditures each year.

As our responsibility for making informed healthcare decisions increases, the existing system is poorly equipped to help us in our new role. In addition, the healthcare system does not always provide incentives for behaviors and choices that will lead to better health and better outcomes. Few resources are spent on addressing our emerging needs: selecting cov-erage that is appropriate for our family's economic, life-stage, and health status; planning for anticipated short- and long-term costs; evaluating resources to keep us healthy; and, ultimately, getting assistance in effectively navigating the care setting when we need to use it.

The consumer life cycle can be broken into four major steps: selecting a plan, managing one's health, accessing care, and seeking assistance with questions. Let's discuss each of these briefly.

1. Selecting a plan. Choosing health coverage may be one of the most important decisions you make each year. The plan you choose determines what care is covered; which doctors, hospitals, and pharmacies are in your network; and how much you will pay when you receive care. The design and packaging of all these items into a product for which you pay a monthly premium is commonly referred to in the industry as a *health benefit plan*. The media and politicians often refer to benefit plans as "health coverage" or "health insurance." As with all products, it is important to understand the features of what you are buying.

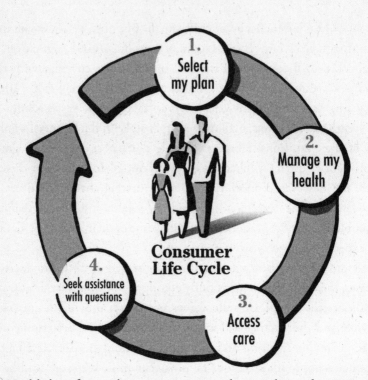

Health benefits are becoming increasingly complex and contain many trade-offs among cost, choice, and coverage. As personal financial responsibility increases, how you save and pay for both short- and long-term healthcare costs becomes as important as the doctor or coverage you choose. Consumers need tools and information for selecting health plans and determining the best way to anticipate and pay for the care they will use. However, the little information that is available is often on paper or in other formats that make comparison difficult. Today, many of us feel we must make our best guess among our alternatives and hope that things work out.

Selecting and enrolling in a health plan is a multistep process and varies slightly based on whether your coverage is employer sponsored, purchased directly from your health plan, or arranged through a government-sponsored plan such as Medicare or Medicaid. If you get your health insurance through an employer, the employer generally provides education regarding benefit options and cost trade-offs. If you purchase health insurance directly, your health plan or broker provides that information. To help navigate the enormous volume of information about health coverage options, employers and health plans might provide online tools to guide you in making decisions. Some might even offer you the ability to enroll online in the plan of your choice so you don't have to deal with cumbersome forms. Healthcare reform legislation passed in 2010 calls for the creation of *health exchanges* that will enable healthcare consumers who purchase health insurance directly to compare prices for similar benefit plans from a variety of health plans in an online marketplace and then enroll directly in the plan they choose. Given the widespread use of the Internet, all health plans will probably improve their abilities to clearly present benefit plans to you (whether you purchase health insurance directly or through your employer)—similar to the way in which online retailers such as Amazon present the features of their products. Once you enroll, your health plan typically sends you an ID card, which signals that you have health insurance and are officially eligible to receive care.

2. **Managing your health.** Managing your health, and that of your family members, has different meanings depending upon your health status. If you are generally healthy, it is about prevention and being able to make good healthcare decisions regarding exercise, nutrition, and other daily activities that keep you out of the doctor's office. A rapidly increasing number of Americans are at increased risk for illnesses such as diabetes or heart disease. For them, staying healthy might mean following the doctor's recommended changes to diet and exercise as well as regularly taking prescribed medications to help delay or prevent the onset of disease. For people who have developed disease, staying healthy means doing the best they can to slow the progression of (or even reverse) the condition they have developed. The fact is that we as consumers perform most of the activities related to staying well (roughly 80 percent) right in the comfort of our own homes.[2]

To help you stay healthy, you need effective online tools, services, and information about key aspects of your health. Consumers (and their doctors) are increasingly turning to general search sites such as Google or Bing to look up health information, as well as to healthcare-specific sites such as WebMD. Numerous blogs also provide a forum for more in-depth discussion on health topics and can help to answer patient questions not answered during a time-pressured doctor visit. Consumers need to be aware that search results and blogs, depending upon the quality of the source, can contain inaccurate or misleading information. It is always best to consult your physician or health plan if you are unsure. More recently, social networks like Twitter and Facebook allow for discussion forums with people of like interests, although it is sometimes uncomfortable for people to openly discuss or broadcast their personal healthcare issues. You should expect the development of healthcare-specific social networking environments, such as Caféwell, that will ensure that consumers can control how their privacy needs are met while also being able to connect with common-interest groups, their health plans, and their providers in innovative ways. You will even see the combining of online education and online social gaming, where consumers can save money toward paying for their healthcare by playing games or participating in activities that help them learn more about their health status and conditions. With these types of social media, more people than ever before will be able to educate themselves about health topics, and the people and organizations constructing these online tools will get better at ensuring that the content and information are coordinated with your benefits and care.

Unfortunately, when it comes to determining what information sources we can trust to keep ourselves healthy today, we receive virtually no systematic guidance from the healthcare system, so it is up to each of us to research and make sense of the overwhelming amount of information on the Internet and from well-meaning friends and relatives. Once you are enrolled in a health plan, today's system largely ignores you until you eventually do seek care, triggering a chain of financial and administrative tasks, such as claims and customer service inquiries, that historically have been the focus of health plans. However, there is growing attention and effort being focused on determining how health plans and providers can become more effective "partners in health" with their members and patients. In keeping with the old adage "An ounce of prevention is worth a pound of cure," many employers and health plans are zeroing in on wellness and prevention as well as chronic disease management as ways to reduce rising costs and create healthier employees. Examples of wellness and prevention initiatives are discounts on fitness club memberships, workplace exercise classes, classes on how to quit smoking, and the addition of low-calorie or low-sodium menu items in company cafeterias. Chronic disease management programs include weight management or diabetes management programs that employ health coaches to check in with consumers and help them accomplish health goals. Consumers need to know how these programs can help them take control of their health and how to access available programs.

3. Accessing care. Going to the doctor or the hospital is something many of us dread. Choosing the right doctor, setting up the appointment, filling out the repetitive paper forms, waiting to be examined, and dealing with the barrage of associated paperwork from the doctor and your health plan all make the hassle factor seem overwhelming. Before, during, and after we receive healthcare, we are often ill equipped to make good decisions. Before going to the doctor's office, do you have at your fingertips your medical history, prescriptions, and health profile information? Do you know which doctors are in your health plan's network of participating doctors, whether your visit will be covered, and if so, how much it will cost you? While there, do you clearly understand your treatment options and the potential trade-offs among cost, quality, and effectiveness for the choices you have to make? When you leave, do you know how much you will be charged for the services you just received, and do you have an agreed-upon follow-up plan with your doctor beyond "Take two aspirins and call me in the morning"? These pieces of information must be made available to both patients and their doctors before, during, and after care is delivered. Only with shared or "transparent" information about cost and care options will patients be able to make better-informed decisions.

4. Seeking assistance with questions. As healthcare consumers, we often have questions about our benefits and care. Today, we typically contact our health plan only for administrative issues such as ordering a replacement ID card, changing demographic data such as address or phone number, or inquiring about the virtually unintelligible paperwork we received in the mail related to our last doctor visit. As our responsibilities increase—requiring us to make decisions about coverage options, how to pay for healthcare, and where to seek care—we have new needs for support, and we have new questions. To whom will we turn for assistance? While many people indicate they don't have complete trust in health plans, health plans are the best source of truth for many of these questions. How equipped is your doctor to answer these types of questions? While it may not seem obvious today, many health plans are going through a transformation to be able to better support consumers through these increasingly complex decisions. For many consumers, a health coach (a healthcare professional who helps you meet goals for fitness, weight loss, and other health goals) or healthcare financial planning specialist (someone who gives advice about how to save for and pay for healthcare expenses) is just a phone call away. Health plans are beginning an evolution that I believe will be very similar to the evolution that the financial services/banking industry underwent in the 1990s. If you can remember a time when banks were open only from nine o'clock in the morning to five o'clock in the afternoon, Monday through Friday, ask yourself if you could have foreseen a time when these same banks, which did little more than process checks, make loans, and mail us monthly statements, would evolve into full-service financial planning and services companies, with around-the-clock, technology-enabled customer service and support?

Healthcare through the Eyes of Providers: Doctors, Hospitals, and Pharmacies

From the time we are young, many of us dream of becoming doctors, nurses, or other medical professionals. Health professionals must invest a tremendous amount of time and money in order to receive the education and training necessary for their chosen specialty. As a result, they have a very real need to earn a livelihood that justifies the time and money they have invested in their education and training. The American Medical Association estimates that medical students owe, on average, $140,000 for student loans upon graduation.[3] This enormous debt is one reason some medical students look to the greener pastures of specialty care, where they are often better compensated.[4]

While they have been trained in the science of medicine, providers are often unprepared for the incredibly complex business side of healthcare. Ultimately, the money collected for delivering care needs to be sufficient to fund operations and provide an appropriate level of profit. Revenues must be sufficient to pay the medical professionals and office staff, cover the rent and the cost of malpractice insurance, buy supplies and equipment, and maintain the technology providers need to deliver care and manage the business. This business reality may have a direct impact on the experience of patients when they get care. For example, if you have ever felt that your time with your physician was rushed, your doctor may have been attempting to balance her desire to spend time with you against real economic pressures to see as many patients as possible each day. As the saying goes, "Time is money." In today's healthcare system, it is virtually impossible for most providers, particularly those in smaller settings, to separate the science of practicing medicine from the business of being reimbursed for care.

Like consumers, providers also have a life cycle that accounts for their interactions with the health plan as well as with the patients they treat. The four primary steps in the life cycle are as follows: contracting with health plans, scheduling/preparing for patient visits, providing care, and getting paid.

1. Contracting with the health plan. When providers deliver goods or services, they have two sources of income: you (the patient) and, for those patients who have health coverage, the health plan. How much they are paid by a health plan for a specific procedure is determined by a negotiated "fee schedule" contract between the provider and the plan. This price negotiation process is an incredibly important part of the provider life cycle, as it sets the financial criteria that will drive the provider's economic success. In most parts of the country, one provider may have contracts with a dozen or more health plans, as well as with Medicare and Medicaid. That is a dozen or more negotiations and a dozen or more different agreements for payment for each different procedure, introducing administrative complexity that will have ripple effects throughout your experience as a patient. It is common to hear doctors and hospitals complain about the rates they are reimbursed by private health plans. However, in almost all cases, Medicare and Medicaid pay less. We will explore the economics of the healthcare system in the next chapter, but it is important for you to understand that providers are under great pressure to ensure they get paid enough to run their practice or facility and still make a reasonable income.

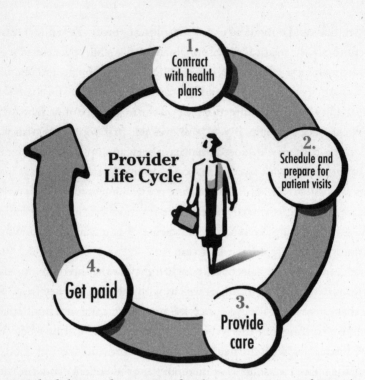

2. Scheduling and preparing for the patient visit. Before each patient visit, providers must validate the patient's eligibility for healthcare coverage and gather any relevant medical history. Today, much of this process is manual. We are all too familiar with providing our medical background by filling out the forms on the clipboard. It is important to remember that in many cases, providers work in a cottage industry in that they have little technological support around them to help them share information.

When it comes to your patient medical history, providers have a blind spot. They are dependent upon information you as a patient volunteer, as well as whatever information exists within your "chart"—the history of your care within that medical practice. Doctors have very little ability to access data outside of that care setting, such as information from other physicians you have seen, lab and imaging tests you have had, or medications you are taking. Providers express a tremendous desire for automation in this and other areas. Increasingly, health plans are enabling real-time access to information about patient eligibility, medical history, treatment plans, and patient financial responsibility at the point of service. There are substantial national efforts under way for both physician offices and hospitals to capture and distribute clinical information in electronic health records that can communicate with one another, but it will be many years before that goal is fully realized. Another movement afoot is an effort to create a personal health record for every patient in the United States. Such a health record would contain historical information about all the treatments a patient has received from all providers. In the immediate term, the most practical and broad-based "patient record" for people who do not receive care in an integrated delivery system (which typically has a common set of electronic records) is a personal health record where the information is provided by health insurance companies. This type of personal health record contains your health history including your past diagnoses, procedures you have undergone, the dates and places of these services, your treating physician, and your prescription history. The reason such a record is a good solution for right now is that the data are already stored in computers (instead of in paper files), and the information systems of private payers already are capable of sharing it with the patient and provider.

3. Providing care. During the visit, doctors must balance the pressure to see more patients with the desire to spend the time to diagnose and treat each one. Thanks to the Internet, you and I can find dozens of sites to help us diagnose and form an opinion about which care option is best for us. Imagine, as a doctor, having to deal with dozens of self-diagnosed patients each day. While it is commendable that patients want to come prepared to the doctor's visit, the danger is that patients sometimes latch onto treatment options that are not covered under their particular health benefits package or that might be ineffective or dangerous given the patient's individual health status, age, or medical condition. Providers also face more pressure from private and government payers to follow evidence-based medicine guidelines throughout the care process. In addition, primary care doctors face a proliferation of substitute services. For example, clinics staffed by nurses or nurse practitioners are now located in large discount retailers that also have in-house pharmacies. These clinics are able to provide common diagnostic tests (such as checking for strep throat) and then prescribe the

antibiotic to be filled on-site, and they can typically administer flu vaccinations. Another example is that some employers offer similarly staffed corporate clinics that can provide the same services without the patient ever having to leave her work site. Finally, there are hybrid health plan models where, although the patient normally receives care from his own primary care physician and local specialists, once certain health conditions arise (such as a hospitalization for a respiratory or circulatory problem), from that point on the patient's care is managed by the health plan's own physicians (sometimes called *intensivists*). This change alters the relationship between the primary care doctor and the patient and may make it harder for the primary care doctor to coordinate the patient's care and be reimbursed.

Perhaps the biggest change doctors face is that in addition to treating illness, they are increasingly being asked to take a broader role in improving or preventively maintaining the health status of their patients. Their world is changing from one where they have taken care of patients mainly in their own medical offices and local hospitals to one where they must keep track of the care their patients receive in a variety of care settings. They must spend time reviewing their own patient data to proactively plan how to improve the health status of their entire population of patients, such as by making sure preventive tests are administered on a timely basis. Managing their patient populations includes referring patients to participate in prevention and wellness programs such as obesity management and smoking cessation. Even the definition of a "visit" is changing, as doctors are beginning to consult with their patients by phone or the web. Naturally, doctors want to be paid for these evolving technology-related services, which are often referred to as "tele-medicine."

4. Getting paid. As we touched on in the beginning of this section and in greater detail in chapter 4, the amount providers are reimbursed by health plans is usually based upon the number of "procedures" (such as a routine checkup, a follow-up exam, or a removal of stitches) a physician "produces" (or performs) in a particular setting and the "price" that is collected for each procedure. Sounds simple enough, right? However, few people understand how complex this system actually is: the amount received for a particular procedure, and who will pay it, varies from patient to patient based upon the health insurance plan (and the contracting process we discussed in step 1 of the provider life cycle). Imagine running a business where the price of your product or service varies for each customer. Now imagine that neither you nor your customer knows the price or who is going to pay for the good or service until days, weeks, or months after it is provided or consumed. Such is the case in healthcare.

As patients become responsible for more and more of the cost of physician payment in today's high-deductible benefit plans, doctors face new business problems. Without accurate information about who pays what share of a procedure or office visit (i.e., the patient's liability versus the health plan's liability), the practice may not realize that the patient is responsible for the majority of the bill. If the provider does not collect the patient's money when care is provided at the point of service, the amount he actually does collect is likely to be less than the amount he is owed because it is difficult, time consuming, and expensive to chase down payments from consumers by using billing services and, in severe cases, collection agencies. The end result of increased patient liability in higher-deductible plans is that, particularly early in each calendar year, providers who do not collect the right amount from patients may not generate enough money coming in to keep up with the cost of running their practices.

The Changing Role of Employers in Health Benefits

As I mentioned at the beginning of this chapter, the majority of Americans who have healthcare insurance obtain their coverage through their employers, who historically have paid the lion's share of the cost of coverage as part of their employees' total compensation package. Employers consider competitive health benefits critical to attracting and retaining a talented workforce and to keeping employees effective and productive in the workplace.

Over the past ten years, healthcare costs have skyrocketed. For employers, offering healthcare coverage has become a significant challenge in an increasingly competitive global market. Because the cost of providing healthcare coverage to employees must ultimately be reflected in the price of the employers' goods and services, employers face tough decisions. Most are proportionately sharing healthcare coverage cost increases with their employees. Many have been forced to reduce the level of coverage they offer, and a growing number cannot afford to offer benefits at all.

While healthcare premiums continue to grow at a rate that is faster than both general inflation and annual wage increases, there has been little demonstrable improvement in the results the healthcare system delivers. Hence, employers are questioning the value they are receiving and have begun to demand more value from the entire healthcare system. The existing health benefits model is largely focused on the administrative processes related to enrolling employees in coverage and processing claims when employees use the system. It does relatively little to help promote health or manage existing illness, which would better address the employer's goal of keeping employees healthy and productive.

Walking in the shoes of an employer throughout the healthcare life cycle is one way to better understand how the affordability crisis is fundamentally changing the employer's role. The employer's life cycle includes four key steps: determining and selecting benefits, enrolling employees, managing employee health, and managing/tracking benefits.

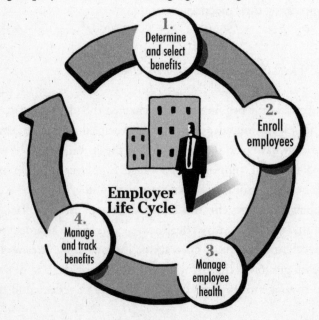

1. Determining and selecting benefits. Health benefits management is a big job. While many large companies have benefits managers, many small businesses outsource benefits management or must take a do-it-yourself approach. Each year, companies must look closely at their health benefits and decide whether to continue with their current health plan relationships and benefit offerings or make changes. One interesting question that has surfaced as a result of healthcare reform legislation is whether employers will stay involved in determining benefit programs for their employees. The legislation imposes a penalty on certain employers who don't either offer health insurance to employees or make a large enough financial contribution toward the cost of their health insurance, but there is speculation that in order to avoid penalties, some employers will simply make financial contributions and will ask their employees to arrange for health insurance themselves. Either method is systematically workable, but it would be an awfully big burden to healthcare consumers if they had to find their own health insurance plans instead of receiving benefit plan assistance from their employers.

Most small and mid-sized employers work with brokers (independent consultants who give advice about what benefits fit the needs of employers and their employees). Larger employers may work directly with brokers or the payers' sales staffs. Together they examine the demographics of the workforce and the financial objectives of the employers. Based upon the size and composition of the workforce, health plans submit proposals they believe meet the benefit level and price point the employer wants or needs. The employer then must decide whether to stay with the existing plan choices or to pick new ones. In general, employers may offer their employees several benefit/price combinations from the chosen health plan, but they rarely offer competing choices from two or more different plans. Once employers have made a choice, they work with the broker or payer to set up the benefits within the health plan's information systems in preparation for the employee enrollment process.

2. Enrolling employees. Once the setup process is completed, it is time to enroll employees in their choice of benefits through a process called *open enrollment*. During this process, employees are educated about the benefit options and any prerequisites such as health risk assessments or health screenings. The administrative tasks and paperwork involved in educating employees on their benefit options and enrolling them and their family members in health benefit plans can be cumbersome for any employer. As a result, many employers have adopted technology solutions that make the employee benefit selection and enrollment processes easier. For example, once the employer has selected a limited number of plans to offer to employees, some health plans may make an online benefits calculator available so that employees can run through a number of scenarios based on their anticipated healthcare needs and find the best fit for their families. Once employees have selected which benefits plan they want from a particular health plan, employers work with the broker or health plan to enter this information into the health plan's information systems, which ultimately produce ID cards that will be delivered to the employees as evidence of health coverage when they go to a doctor or hospital.

3. Managing employee health. Employers provide employee health benefit coverage in order to attract employees and maintain a healthy workforce. After all, healthy employees are more productive and use fewer sick days. Because employee absenteeism costs American companies billions of dollars in lost revenue and productivity, employers are looking for benefit plan designs that promote health and wellness, rather than plans that simply treat illness. In collaboration with their health plans, employers increasingly are providing the information and incentives that employees need to manage their own health more actively. Employers are changing how they view healthcare and are taking action to promote a culture of health. For example, within the workplace, some employers offer fitness centers, health fairs, and cafeterias filled with healthy food options in an effort to promote health and wellness. Others may pay cash rewards to employees who achieve weight loss goals. And some even provide a premium "holiday," waiving a portion of the premium for employees who complete health risk assessments.

4. Managing/tracking benefits. Throughout the course of the year, employers must manage and track the benefits of the company's employees. Any time an employee's status changes, whether it's due to the birth of a child, a move to another location, or even termination of employment, there are implications not only for the employee's eligibility status, but also for the company's premium payments to the health plan. This monthly process of reconciling who is eligible, what premiums are due to the health plan, and what portion of the premium is paid by the employee requires ongoing time and effort. Moreover, the employer's health benefit administrators often act as the first level of customer service, triaging calls from employees who have healthcare questions. Employers need tools to help streamline and manage these processes.

In addition to the monthly reconciliation process, employers track the effectiveness and value of their employee benefit coverage over the course of the year. They ask questions such as "Is our healthcare utilization (the amount of care our employees receive) going up or down? Are employees healthier overall? Are they satisfied with the health plan's service?" When it comes time for the annual contract renewal process, the answers to these questions will help determine whether the employer stays with the same health plan or shops for a new one. Ultimately, employers need benefit designs that help slow the rate of premium growth or even reduce the cost of providing healthcare coverage. Sadly, if real progress is not made regarding the value delivered by the healthcare system, employers will be compelled to minimize their role, perhaps even washing their hands of selecting and funding health benefits. If employers become less involved, more consumers will find themselves in the middle of the healthcare jungle with one fewer advocate to help them navigate.

Brokers Enable Effective Distribution of Health Benefits

Earlier in this chapter, we examined the importance of healthcare purchasing decisions in the context of both the employer and the consumer. Brokers play an important role in helping consumers and employers decide which health plan company and what types of benefits will best meet their needs. With more than one million licensed health and life insurance brokers in the nation, they are a big part of the healthcare supply chain.[5]

Most people are familiar with auto insurance brokers, commonly known as insurance agents. Healthcare brokers are similar, but they bring health benefit buyers and sellers together. They earn their customers (individuals and employers) by offering competitive health benefit products from health plans and by providing services that assist with the selection, enrollment, and ongoing support of the chosen health benefit products.

Brokers are paid a commission by the health plans in exchange for the "book of business" (the roster of insured lives) they deliver and for the services they provide to support their clients. Essentially, brokers are an extension of both the sales force and the customer service units of the health plan. Ultimately, brokers want to sell competitive products from health plans that deliver high levels of quality and service. And they want their customers to renew their contracts with their existing health plans so brokers do not have to repeat the costly selection/replacement process on a frequent basis.

The life cycle of brokers parallels that of employers and includes four key responsibilities: evaluating and selecting health plans, educating and enrolling employees, advocating employee health, and managing service and costs.

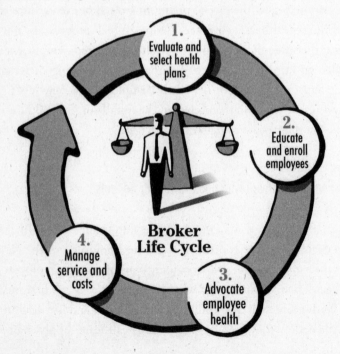

1. Evaluating and selecting the health plan. Brokers want products that meet their clients' needs, which include health and wellness coverage at a reasonable cost. While cost is a big factor in whether brokers will recommend a particular health plan to their employer clients, brokers usually do not recommend health plans based on cost alone. Rather, brokers look for health plans that can differentiate themselves in several ways. Specifically, they look for benefit plan designs that drive down medical costs, information technology tools that reduce paperwork, and service offerings (such as health coaches) that will enhance customer satisfaction. Evaluating and selecting the right health plan for an employer requires that brokers understand not only the plan's benefit offering, but also the tools and services the health plan provides to help control costs and improve customer satisfaction. Brokers ultimately drive more business to those health plans that do a good job of educating and collaborating with them and with consumers, as well as providing the tools that make the selling process easier. For example, I mentioned earlier that some health plans provide benefits calculators to help consumers pick the plans that best fit their needs. Some health plans can fill in data about their treatments and costs from previous years so that a consumer can use these tools to run through some "what if" scenarios. For example, a consumer might ask, "What if I had picked this plan last year? How much would I have spent out of pocket versus with a different plan?" Further, brokers encourage health plans to neatly package explanations of benefits in both paper and online forms so they are easy for the broker to distribute. Also, by sending e-mails with the right link to the health plan's website, brokers help arrange for the easy connection between the health plan's online enrollment capabilities and the employees who need to sign up. In addition, brokers send reminders to employees about completing the enrollment process. These examples of brokers' services apply to new sales as well as renewals of existing contracts, which require less effort by brokers than starting from scratch. Brokers tend to develop ongoing relationships with those health plans that can deliver the best combination of benefit plan products, tools, and ease of distribution in the geographic areas they cover—or, in the case of a national broker, those health plans that have products that can serve employees in multiple states.

2. Educating and enrolling employees. In order to increase their chances of renewing existing contracts, brokers need to provide excellent service to their customers. To this end, they need tools that streamline enrollment and help consumers choose providers based on data about quality. Online enrollment capabilities reduce the administrative burden for employers by eliminating paper application forms and often serve as a way to educate employees about trade-offs. One example of such a trade-off is for a fairly healthy person (who does not tend to require many medical services) to select a plan with higher co-payments but with a lower premium amount. Brokers also look at how to get employees to enroll in disease management programs (such as classes for managing diabetes) and health and wellness programs (such as weight management and fitness) when employees are signing up for their health plan so they can benefit from these programs from the very beginning.

3. Advocating employee health. In addition to helping employers navigate their choices and select and enroll in a health plan, brokers increasingly seek to play the role of employee advocate, offering assistance in promoting a culture of health. For example, brokers have become more involved in monitoring trends within the employer's employee population. Are people getting healthier? Are they using more healthcare services or fewer? Are employees participating in available health and wellness programs? If not, why not? The answers to questions such as these play a key role in helping employers decide how to modify next year's benefit design and health plan.

4. Managing service and costs. The work of a broker, like that of an employer, does not stop once employees are enrolled in the health plan. Brokers spend their time after enrollment monitoring the status of their accounts, including costs, utilization levels (how many units of care and which types of units are used), and customer satisfaction. To that end, brokers depend on reporting tools for each of their accounts. They also provide ongoing service to their employer accounts, including solving billing, eligibility, and claims problems. They add value by doing the legwork for their clients and making sure those clients get the most from their coverage after they've bought it. Many employers choose to bear some or all of the financial risk for the actual cost paid to doctors, hospitals, pharmacies, and other entities for their employees' care, even though the health plan or insurance company has arranged the health benefit plan and provides services. When an employer has chosen this type of self-funded plan, brokers periodically review whether the actual amount being spent on healthcare is consistent with the employer's expectations and budget.

Health Plans as Supply Chain Facilitators

Although health plans are sometimes publicly maligned as heartless corporations, some people lose sight of the fact that health plans are managed and operated by human beings who are as intent on providing high-quality healthcare to the members of their plans as are the doctors, nurses, and other providers who deliver the care. One common measure of a health plan's success is how many members belong to it—or, alternatively stated, how many people choose the health plan's products. A health plan product typically consists of a defined set of benefit options (with accompanying deductible and co-insurance levels), a price, health management services and restrictions (such as where you can go to get which services), and administrative services (such as claims payment and customer service). This definition of a health plan product is the same regardless of whether you select and enroll directly (either through a broker or through an online exchange), or you sign up for a health plan offered by your employer.

As we saw in chapter 4, supply chains—whether in retail or in healthcare—must be assembled and managed by someone; organizing your own healthcare supply chain from the Yellow Pages or from online sources that are not coordinated is frustrating and difficult. For those of us with health insurance, our health plans organize the healthcare supply chain for us. They interact with all the healthcare constituents—consumers, providers, employers, and brokers. By developing strong enterprise information systems for services and support so that all these constituents have consistent information (such as who is eligible and what benefits are covered), and by offering products that meet these constituents' needs, health plans can help consumers, providers, employers, and brokers work together during each step of the life cycles described earlier. Let's take a look on a basic level at what health plans do and the types of issues they face as they attempt to organize our healthcare supply chain. Within the health plan's own life cycle, there are eight key business processes that support and facilitate the healthcare supply chain:

Product development means designing the health benefit "products" that will be priced and offered to consumers via employers and brokers, or directly on a retail basis. One example of a health benefit product is a high-deductible plan with a health savings account. Another example sold directly to consumers is a Medicare Advantage plan (a supplemental plan for people age sixty-five and older that typically provides additional benefits that are not covered by traditional Medicare).

Risk management is the process of figuring out how to price various health benefit products so that the health plan (or self-funded employer group) that takes on risk for a population of people can remain solvent. In other words, the pricing of health insurance premiums for a given plan design has to be enough to pay the doctors, hospitals, pharmacies, and other entities for the services they provide while maintaining adequate reserves of money that are usually regulated by government agencies.

Revenue management includes the processes to support health benefit sales, employer group setup, member enrollment, and the ongoing collection of premiums, either from employers or individuals. When you receive your ID card that shows you are eligible for health benefits, that is how you (and any providers who might treat you) know that you are enrolled in a health plan. Typically, employer groups and individuals are billed monthly for insurance premiums, and these payments are recorded in order to maintain your eligibility to receive health plan benefits.

Customer service means providing ongoing support and assistance to consumers, providers, employers, and brokers throughout each step in their respective life cycles (which were described earlier in this chapter). For example, health plans help answer questions consumers might have about whether a particular service or type of treatment is covered; they might give providers information about whether a particular patient is still covered (eligible) under a particular plan; and they might answer employers' questions about whether their employees are incurring fewer claims based upon an injury prevention program that has been implemented. There are countless other examples of the support and assistance health plans offer to consumers, providers, employers, and brokers, and there are few industries in which the different types of constituents and the issues they need addressed are so varied and complex.

Reimbursement management includes making sure claims are paid quickly and accurately so that physicians, hospitals, and pharmacies are reimbursed for care they have provided. In order to reimburse providers accurately, health plans must determine how much money the consumer owes for each service provided and how much the health plan (payer) must pay directly to the providers. Before any payment is made to the provider, the payer must make sure the service is covered under the consumer's benefit plan. The reimbursement management process is complete when the consumer has paid the amount he owes and the health plan has reimbursed the provider properly for the amount it owes.

Care management means managing health both for "populations" (e.g., whether all health plan members over forty years old are getting the recommended preventive tests in a timely manner) and for individuals (e.g., whether you are getting access to evidence-based care for your sports injury). Health plans assist consumers in seeking and providers in delivering effective and appropriate care. Care management techniques include patient education, distribution of evidence-based medicine guidelines, disease management campaigns (e.g., helping diabetics stay as healthy as possible), and case management for complex injury and illness situations (such as when someone suffers a stroke and requires immediate rehabilitation to regain the greatest amount of physical and mental function possible). Sometimes, care management can mean preventing unnecessary care or imposing care guidelines to reduce unwarranted variation in care, often referred to as utilization management.

Network management includes contracting with all providers on the supply side to create a provider network (doctors, hospitals and other medical facilities, diagnostic centers, and pharmacies) that has been approved by a health plan, and to agree to provide care at pre-arranged prices to members. In this process, the health plan verifies the credentials of providers, negotiates pricing (typically discounted) on behalf of members and employers, and may also monitor the quality of services being provided in order to maintain a high-value network.

Finance and administration include internal financial processes (such as accounting for all the premium revenue taken in and all the claims payments sent out); legal and regulatory processes (e.g., making sure health benefit plans comply with laws and that sales processes are not misleading); developing and maintaining sophisticated information technology systems; and the people, offices, and equipment necessary to do the financial and administrative work of the health plan.

While these processes provide a snapshot of how most health plans organize the healthcare supply chain now, they are constantly changing as pressure to improve quality and reduce cost in particular areas increases. For example, over the past decade, health plans have focused largely on driving down administrative costs within their operations. Widespread investment in technology to efficiently enroll members and pay claims has been a top priority and has returned impressive results. However, as the cost of care delivery continues to increase, many health plans have begun to see care management as an area in which they can increasingly help to manage cost and quality. For example, health plans are seeking better ways to share information with doctors about the health history and pharmacy history of patients (e.g., notifying doctors when their patients have failed to refill a preventive prescription) and working to design programs where doctors and patients can more easily collaborate in following care guidelines.

As health plans once again try to manage the cost and quality of care, they are well aware of the challenge they face this time around. They must use those principles of managed care that worked in the late 1980s and early

1990s to improve quality and reduce costs, but do so in a way that educates consumers, providers, employers, and brokers and encourages them to become partners with health plans, rather than adversaries. Managed care in the 1980s and 1990s proved costs can be effectively controlled; however, the restrictions on convenience and choice were so unpalatable to many people that managed care as a whole was rejected. And yet, providers, employers, and government policy makers acknowledge that the managed care concepts of population management (such as segmentation) and organized networks of care providers make sense today. It is important to note that any type of entity that is responsible for caring for a population of people within a budgeted amount (such as accountable care organizations) will have to perform most, if not all, of the functions of a health plan. Finding the right balance of managed care principles is the key to solving this difficult but doable systems challenge.

Because today's health plans interact with all parts of the healthcare system; understand the life cycles of consumers, providers, employers, and brokers; and have experience managing both information systems and large populations of people, they are in an ideal position to contribute to the design of a better system. By developing incentives for consumers and providers that promote improved health and by using information systems to help people make informed decisions about their benefits and care, our healthcare system will be able to provide better care for less money—an accomplishment all Americans would welcome.

As you will learn in the next chapter, a wealth of information that can add value to the healthcare experience exists in the physical and electronic files and databases of consumers, providers, payers, employers, and brokers. The challenge is that much of it is stored in fragmented silos, with no easy way to share information among these constituents.

Chapter 6

Information Silos:
A Fragmented System

Knowledge is like money: to be of value, it must circulate, and in circulation it can increase in quantity, and hopefully in value.
—Louis L'Amour, *Education of a Wandering Man*, 1989

D o you have a club card for your favorite supermarket chain? If you do, you know that no matter which location you visit, the system knows you—giving you your frequent-shopper discount and crediting points to your account. In addition, at checkout time you likely receive coupons for items you have bought in the past or for competing products in the same category, based on promotional agreements the store negotiated with various manufacturers and distributors. These stores do a good job of systematically collecting data about you, such as your past purchases, spending levels, and method of payment. They also know your address, zip code, and phone number. They combine these data into useful information that allows them to customize offers intended to create value for you and build loyalty.

Believe it or not, the US healthcare system collects far more data about you than does your supermarket. Yet most supermarket chains do a better job than our healthcare system of using this information to conveniently serve consumers. What is behind this difference? In our healthcare system, much of the collected data are locked up in *information silos* and neither shared with the people who need it nor combined with other information to unlock the data's full power. Just as each farm stores its own grain in an individual silo, each doctor's office, hospital, imaging center, and other healthcare provider collects data about you and your family, uses it quickly for one or two transactions (such as to process your claim or issue your ID card), and then stores it in a computer or file cabinet. That data might never be used again.

Redundancy: The Biggest Irritant in Healthcare

Perhaps the most obvious example of how information silos affect you is the insidious paper form that you are asked to complete every time you see a different doctor or go to an emergency room. In this age of technology, when a retailer can take information you supply and use it to recognize you every time you enter any branch of the store, it is hard to believe the healthcare system is not set up to share basic information contained on an intake form, particularly if you have health insurance. Imagine what it would be like if you could complete a detailed, carefully developed form once, preferably online, and this information could be made available throughout the healthcare system as appropriate. Not only is it annoying and inefficient to have to complete the same form over and over, but the fact that important information is not being shared and used to its full potential is both expensive and dangerous.

As mentioned earlier, legislation has made funds available for doctors to develop and use electronic health records in their practices to digitally store information. (We'll talk more about electronic health records in chapter 9.) But this provider-only approach, while helpful to the important issue of patient safety, will take a decade to achieve a meaningful impact on solving the issues of healthcare cost and overall quality. This is because the electronic health record being developed is based on activities that go on in clinical settings but fails to systematically connect all the supply chain elements we learned about in chapter 4 and the constituents (consumers, providers, employers, and brokers) we learned about in chapter 5. Nor will it necessarily deliver helpful cost transparency for various medical services and procedures. As we all know, it takes time to integrate people, processes, and technology. (Remember my earlier comment on paving cow paths:

simply digitizing a fragmented system will not fix it.) But despite the long lead time for implementation, it is clear that electronic health records are a move in the right direction. Obviously, when your supermarket knows more about you simply from your phone number than does the healthcare system in spite of your many interactions with it, something needs to change.

Information Silo Basics

Without overcomplicating the issue, data assembled to accomplish something useful are "information." For example, when a store's information technology analyzes your shopping history (the data) against available coupon promotions, the result is useful information about what type of coupon to print on the back of your grocery receipt. Information scientists also talk about knowledge (applying what is learned from information) and wisdom (knowing when seemingly good information or conventional knowledge is faulty or out of context). For purposes of this chapter, we will use the term "information" to represent the broader spectrum.

As we learned in chapter 4, there are more than 250 million people in the United States who receive health coverage in either organized systems of payments and care or organized systems of benefits and care, and that number is likely to increase as a result of healthcare reform legislation. Our healthcare system has large amounts of information about each person. However, unlike a supermarket, our healthcare system stores its information in silos, meaning that each group of information cannot easily be combined with the others because it exists in a multitude of computer databases and paper-based files that are not linked together. As we saw in chapter 1, the information silos in healthcare fall into three main areas: core benefit administration, care management, and constituent information.

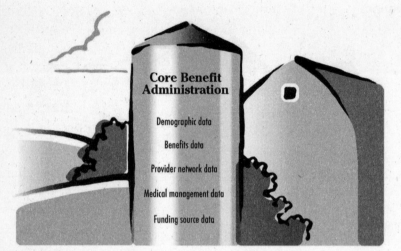

The Core Benefit Administration Silo: Demographics, Benefits, Provider Networks, Medical Management, and Funding Sources

This group of information has to do with benefits and other data a health plan collects to keep track of your health benefits or how your care is paid for. *Demographic data* include your name, age, address, other family members covered by your health plan, and other basic facts. *Benefits data* include your employer, your covered health benefits, your insurance premium amount, your claims history (including your diagnoses, procedures you have received to date, and where, when, and by whom the procedures were performed), your prescription drug history, and a host of other data, including how much of the cost gets paid for by you (out of pocket) versus by the health insurer. *Provider network data* keep track of which doctors, hospitals, diagnostic centers, and pharmacies are "in network," along with the precontracted pricing for each type of service or therapy. *Medical management data* supplement benefits data and keep track of which benefits you are able to access on your own and which benefits require additional permissions (or referrals). *Funding source data* include the types of funding mechanisms each consumer can use to help pay for healthcare, whether through pretax dollars such as health savings accounts (HSAs) and flexible spending accounts (FSAs) or through healthcare subsidies available from government agencies such as the State Children's Health Insurance Program (SCHIP). Though funding sources vary, they are the means by which consumers are able to pay for healthcare.

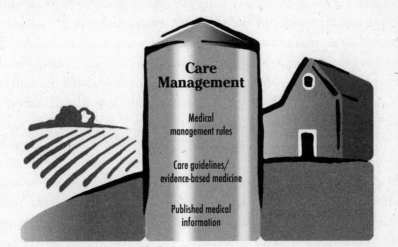

The Care Management Silo:
Rules, Protocols, and Information to Support High-Quality Care

The second silo of information is called care management. This category consists of data intended to ensure that you receive high-quality care. It includes the rules and guidelines established by your health plan (called *medical management rules*) to determine under which circumstances care will be covered (see examples below). The care management silo also contains the documented best practices, the treatment shown by peer-reviewed research to be most effective for various medical conditions (also called *care guidelines* or *evidence-based medicine*). Finally, this information silo contains additional medical information needed to assist you and your doctor in making good decisions about managing your care (called *published medical information*). This additional medical information includes clear, consumer-friendly descriptions of symptoms, diagnoses, and treatments, as well as explanations of the possible side effects of medications. The care management information silo is both scientifically and politically explosive. The body of evidence-based science grows at an astonishing rate and is constantly changing as each new drug is approved, new devices or surgical techniques are developed, and, increasingly, as advancing science teaches us how to evaluate the efficacy of one treatment versus another at the individual genetic level. Discussion about when to enforce the use of scientific evidence-based guidelines in the practice of medicine by physicians with many years of training and experience has created tension and continues to cause payers and providers to challenge one another as to who should determine what is appropriate.

Let's make the care management silo of information clearer by looking at some examples. The medical management rules issued by health plans determine certain guidelines for care for which a provider will be reimbursed. For example, your primary care doctor is authorized by the health plan to evaluate and monitor your overall health and make referrals to specialists when appropriate, but he is not authorized to perform a hip replacement or prescribe an experimental drug. Similarly, your dermatologist is not authorized to perform a kidney transplant. Medical management rules also affect your cost of receiving care at various care settings. For example, you generally pay a moderate co-payment if you have your sore throat treated at your doctor's office or at a retail clinic; however, if you go to the emergency room for a bad cold or a sore throat, you will usually be charged much more out-of-pocket because emergency rooms are one of the most expensive places to receive care. The mailing you received when you enrolled in your health plan probably warned you that the emergency room is for emergencies only. Have you read your health plan's information packet? Do you know the rules your health plan uses to decide whether care will be covered? Do you know if your health plan requires you to get advance permission (called precertification) before you have surgery or certain expensive tests? Some health plans communicate these rules very clearly, while others do not do as good a job explaining these rules and reminding us about them. Similarly, some consumers read their health plan information from cover to cover, while others don't even open the envelope or visit the health plan's website, which contains the same explanations. One reason for today's soaring healthcare costs is consumers' lack of knowledge about the rules for when and where to seek various types of care, combined with few incentives to follow the rules. (We'll talk more about incentives in the next two chapters.)

Evidence-based medicine guidelines are another important part of the care management silo. They are treatment methods that have been developed based on a growing body of peer-reviewed medical research on the comparative effectiveness of various treatments for specific illnesses, conditions, and injuries. One example of an evidence-based recommendation is that people who have diabetes should have an eye exam (including dilation of pupils) at least once a year.[1] Diabetic patients are at risk for retinopathy, an eye disease caused by damage to blood vessels in the eye from high blood glucose levels. Regular eye exams can detect early signs of retinopathy so a patient can receive treatment that might slow the progression of the disease[2] and reduce the likelihood of blindness. However, according to the Dartmouth Atlas of Health Care, guidelines for best practices are not always followed. One study found that fewer than half of all Medicare patients with diabetes received annual eye exams.[3] There are many examples such as this where a relatively simple guideline that could prevent the need for more expensive treatment is not followed consistently. According to the Dartmouth Atlas, this failure to treat patients according to effective care guidelines often tends to occur when more physicians become involved in a patient's care, possibly because it is not clear which doctor is responsible for coordinating the care and because there are no systems to ensure that best practices are followed.[4] Dartmouth Atlas studies also have demonstrated that patients in certain areas of the country receive more tests and treatment than patients in other parts of the country and that in areas where there is a large supply of certain types of services (such as hospitals or expensive diagnostic tests), patients tend to receive more of those services —an interesting fact to keep in mind as you think about how doctors are paid. However, patients who receive *more* services are not necessarily getting *better* care according to recommended guidelines. And in cases such as unnecessary hospitalization, more care can lead to greater risks, such as increased risk of bacterial infection.[5]

You may wonder how it is possible that not all doctors follow evidence-based medicine all the time. Do they simply not have the most up-to-date information? Is it purely a matter of wanting to be paid for ordering extra tests? Or is there more to it? This is a complicated question, but keep in mind the following thoughts: First, doctors are often overwhelmed by the high volume of patients they must see each day, and even though most doctors conscientiously read medical journals and participate in continuing education, it is challenging to translate this knowledge into the daily operations of their practices. For example, in order to integrate new evidence-based guidelines into daily practice, the checklists and procedures that nurses and office staff rely on may need to be updated (either in paper form or within electronic record systems), medical coding and billing procedures may need to be changed to reflect new evidence-based guidelines, and doctors may need to update the educational information they give to patients. A second reason evidence-based medicine guidelines might not find their way into your doctor's practice is that most doctors are trained in scientific methods and may not individually agree on the validity of someone else's research. However, even for those guidelines that nearly all doctors can agree on, the best practice updates doctors receive often are not widely distributed in a format they can access right away or use to communicate efficiently with their patients.

Contrast these doctors with Lexus® technicians, who can access historical records as well as the recommended treatment protocols (including parts and pricing) to repair or perform preventive maintenance on automobiles. Doctors and patients need clear information about what the best approach is, given the patient's diagnosis, medical history, life stage, and other information. In cases where there are several possible approaches or procedures, they need to be able to compare the potential risks and rewards of each course of treatment. The lack of clear and understandable information has resulted in a high degree of variation in medical practice, outcomes, and cost. Moreover, if patients do not understand why one medical approach has been shown to be more effective for their particular situation than another procedure they found on the Internet, they might think their doctor or health plan is denying them that care simply to save money, rather than because the procedure in question has not been shown to be as effective in patients with similar medical histories and of comparable age and health status.

In addition to medical management rules and evidence-based protocols, there is other medical information that completes the care management information silo. One example is printed or web-based healthcare content that can educate and assist you in making informed decisions. Of course, surfing the web on your own can sometimes lead to more confusion than clarity. First of all, it is difficult to tell a reliable information source from an advertisement, blog, or random doctor who simply wishes to express her own opinion about a particular form of treatment. Second, while general information about a condition or disease can be useful background, information about your own healthcare will help you most if it is put into the context of your specific benefit plan and your particular provider network. After all, what good is knowing that a treatment or procedure exists if you don't know if that treatment would be covered by your benefit plan or whether it would be appropriate for someone who takes the prescriptions you take? But health information in the context of your medical history and benefits plan is a valuable type of information in the care management silo.

This would be a good time to mention that vast amounts of data exist in care settings themselves, such as physician offices and hospitals. These facilities have a broad variety of clinical information systems to aid in the practice of medicine and the delivery of care to patients. Some examples of these data are radiology images, laboratory results, and records of medications that have been dispensed. Sometimes silos exist even within a single hospital or doctor's office. In these cases, the need to share information among different departments within the hospital and with doctors and patients is obvious if we are to improve healthcare. As we will see later, information that is not shared among the different stakeholders can promote misaligned incentives in the healthcare system among healthcare constituents.

The Constituent Information Silo: Data about Consumers, Providers, Employers, and Brokers

The third information silo is called constituent information. It includes unique, descriptive information that is captured or inferred about an entity within the healthcare system—whether a consumer, provider, employer, or broker. In a system such as healthcare, with its millions of consumers, hundreds of thousands of providers, and countless other stakeholders, this information about preferences, attitudes, and other facts unique to each person or company is key to designing a systematic process that optimizes benefits and care.

In the case of consumers, much of this type of information is contained inside their heads and known to few others. Some examples include information about whether a person lives alone or has people around to help with medical care or transportation; whether she prefers to communicate by cell phone, online, or by mail; and her educational level and income. Doctors have patients with very different sets of needs and constraints. This constituent information can help doctors develop treatment plans that will work best for a particular patient's situation. For example, a thirty-nine-year-old, single, working mother of four who is living just above the income threshold that makes her eligible for Medicaid probably has a particular set of needs regarding the way her care is delivered. She probably needs care for herself and her family at the lowest possible cost, and in order to avoid missing work, she might need to get her care after-hours. She also may prefer to go to a clinic or hospital near her house if she needs to have lab tests done. And she may not have reliable access to computer or cell phone technology as a means of getting health information. In contrast, a twenty-nine-year-old married lawyer with no children probably has fewer constraints as to when and where she can go for care, and cost may not be as much of a factor in determining her treatment. She probably can depend on her spouse in the event she cannot transport herself to a physical therapy appointment or for a lab test. In addition, she very likely relies heavily on her cell phone and computer as means of receiving information and would benefit from tools like online scheduling. A doctor who sees both of these patients and who has accurate constituent information about each person has the opportunity to tailor their respective care plans in ways that not only are most convenient but also have the best chance of being followed.

Although it may be easiest to think about the characteristics of consumers, other types of constituents—providers, employers, and brokers—also have specific characteristics that are useful in creating important systematic improvements. For example, doctors have information about their education, their areas of specialization, what languages they speak, whether they are accepting new patients, their office hours, and whether they provide "web visits" during which patients can talk to them online instead of coming to the office. Brokers can supply information about the languages they speak, the list of health plans for which they are able to provide quotes, and whether they provide any kind of health or wellness services to assist their clients. Employers have information about whether they provide injury prevention and wellness programs and whether they can answer benefits questions or must rely upon brokers for this service. Obviously, you and I do not need all this information all the time, but it is important to know that it exists so the system can be designed to give all of us—consumers, providers, employers, and brokers—the information we need, when and where we need it, throughout our healthcare encounters.

Healthcare Evolution versus Systematic Design

Clearly, a wealth of information in the three information silos is captured and stored every day somewhere in the healthcare system, but it is fragmented and separated instead of being accessible to all who need it. This fragmentation is no surprise given the history of the US healthcare system. As we have seen in previous chapters, the healthcare system has evolved over time. It has shifted from a model in which experienced insurance professionals tried to predict annual costs (and then crossed their fingers in the hope that actual claims submitted by doctors, hospitals, and pharmacies would not exceed the premium amounts charged to consumers) toward an organized supply chain model that has attempted to create a higher degree of predictability of cost and quality.

While we have come a long way since the early days of insurance, we still have a long way to go. There are only small pockets of the whole healthcare system that have been engineered as a system in the same way as a leading auto manufacturer or a big-box retail store. Consequently, information collection and storage has not been systematically designed to support a common set of rules that can be shared among all the types of healthcare constituents—consumers, providers, employers, and brokers. Many managed care organizations have attempted to do just this since the mid-1980s. As we've discussed, however, coordinated change across people, processes, and technologies is challenging. And rather than finding managed care successes that worked in many areas of the country and using them as models for the rest of the country, people found it politically expedient to malign the whole attempt at systematic change. In other words, the baby was thrown out with the bathwater. Because all the constituents have not agreed on a basic common approach, each constituent has structured its own information collection based on the specific tasks it must accomplish—much like the assembly lines that were used by early American automobile manufacturers. For health plans, the goals are to bill the right premium amount to each employer for its employees, to pay out the approved amount for each claim, to issue ID cards, and to respond to questions from consumers. Doctors have the goal of being reimbursed by following health plan rules while also providing the best care possible. Hospitals and pharmacies have structured their information collection and storage around still other goals, as have all of the other healthcare constituents. But there is far too little information shared among these functional areas. For example, employers and brokers need information about whether the wellness programs they have developed are producing better outcomes at lower costs for their employees and clients, respectively. In order to perform this analysis, information from the benefits administration silo (claims history), the care management silo (care guidelines), and the constituent silo (regarding employer and broker health and wellness programs) would need to be shared and combined.

Adding to the fragmented evolution of healthcare is the fact that its constituents are looking at healthcare from different perspectives, as described in chapter 5. Doctors study medicine empirically and are generally not systems designers. Employers are focused on sustaining and growing their businesses, and they want productive, healthy employees at a reasonable cost. Brokers try to bring order to chaos and match consumers and employers to the best plan that fits their budget. And consumers seek access to care when they need it and to coverage to help pay for it. Only private payers (health plans) are weaving together a supply chain of staggering complexity while trying to please all constituents. But as I mentioned earlier, these payers generally get roundly criticized for imposing organizing principles and systematic constraints.

Disconnect between Core Benefit Administration and Care Management

The information silo concept becomes even more obvious once you walk through the door of a waiting room and enter the world of care. In order to provide the best care possible, each doctor, physical therapist, or other healthcare professional ideally needs to know what care has already been administered to the consumer by others. However, if each provider collects and stores consumer health information in an isolated paper medical record (or even in an electronic one), the other providers cannot access important information on medications being taken, prior surgeries, allergic reactions, and chronic health conditions, all of which would help the provider deliver higher-quality care.

For example, if you forget to tell your neurologist that your primary care doctor prescribed sleeping pills for you last week, your neurologist will be missing a critical piece of information in evaluating treatment options. He may recommend one course of treatment based on the assumption that you are not on any other medications, but he might have made a different decision if he had known you were already taking the sleeping pills. It may surprise you to know that your health plan has a prescription benefit management function that keeps a record of every prescription you have filled as well as which doctors wrote the prescriptions. The health plan collects these data in order to accomplish its administrative goal of issuing proper payment for covered services. The problem is that the information is locked up in that administrative silo, and the health plan has never been instructed to share this type of information with other parts of the system that would find it useful, such as the doctor when he is seeing a patient. But as I mentioned earlier, simply making the data available in an electronic record does not solve the problem. The doctor would deliberately have to change his work flow in order for this information to improve the quality of healthcare that he can deliver at a given cost. In a practical sense, if it takes an extra minute out of a ten-minute office visit for a doctor to look up prescription information, that extra time can have a significant impact on the doctor's productivity. However, if work processes were changed so that the nurse already had this information available before the doctor entered the room, then the doctor would be more likely to use the information, and the new process would save the doctor time and improve the quality of care.

Another example of providers of care not having access to important information in the core benefit administration silo came up when I needed a referral to see a specialist. My doctor considered my situation and gave me the names of two highly regarded otolaryngologists (ear, nose, and throat specialists). Knowing the healthcare jungle as I do, I naturally asked the nurse who was calling with the referral to find out whether these specialists were on my health plan's panel of physicians. I knew that because my doctor sees hundreds of patients with many different benefit plans, it would be unlikely that he would know my plan's network of approved providers. It turned out that only one specialist on the list was in my health plan's provider network, and so I went to that doctor. Had I not known to ask, my referral might well have been to a physician who was not part of my plan's provider network, and I would have had to pay much more for the same service. You may not realize that doctors themselves typically do not have information about your health plan's provider network at their fingertips in the exam room, even though that type of information seems invaluable in making sure you receive high-quality care at a precontracted cost. Moreover, most offices do not automatically have someone check if the recommended specialist is in your network, so understanding about information silos is an important way for you to control your healthcare costs.

Earlier in this book, we saw other examples of information not being systematically shared, such as when a patient moves to another state and forgets to have her former doctor send her medical records to a new doctor. We have also learned about the frightening results of an emergency room not having access to a patient's medical record to check for a drug allergy or interaction between a drug already being taken and one that the ER administers. There are countless other examples of serious medical errors and wasted money that occur because information is not shared among the parts of the healthcare system.

A Health Information Aggregator Is Key

Given how important the sharing of information is in receiving good care, it is difficult to believe that most consumers lack a way to keep track of their health histories as they travel through the healthcare system over a lifetime.

After all, we have statements for our bank accounts and investments that provide detailed information on all account activity within a given period of time. Even college students have a record of all of the classes they have taken, their grades, and any withdrawals or incompletes. As a nation, we do an excellent job of keeping track of important information in so many areas of our lives. However, we fall inexcusably short in the one area where we are guaranteed to amass information from birth until death and where tracking and sharing information could make the difference between living and dying.

As I mentioned previously, one important tool that has begun to take root is the personal health record, a record of all the care a patient receives, which can be filled in and updated by the patient's health plan. It can be accessed by the patient and, with permission, by providers and other caregivers whenever and wherever the patient receives care or medical services. The consumer can see his complete health history as well as relevant financial data such as balances in funding source accounts (e.g., health savings accounts or flexible spending accounts) and how much money was used last year, and providers can see prescriptions and procedures that may have been provided by other medical professionals. In some cases, the consumer may be able to update information or make requests for inaccurate information to be updated in a controlled manner. There is much discussion in healthcare policy circles about both personal health records and their close digital cousins, electronic health records, but so far the former have been implemented only on a limited basis. The distinctions between these tools are described further in chapter 9.

Silos Obscure Pricing Information

As the affordability crisis worsens and employers look for new ways to cut costs while continuing to provide health benefits to their employees, more consumers will find themselves having to manage not only their health but also the cost of their healthcare. Those of us who have health plans in which we pay a small co-payment and leave the rest of the cost of our care to our health plans will find that we are a dwindling species. As more employers offer health plans with affordably priced premiums paired with greater consumer responsibility for out-of-pocket costs, consumers will need information about the actual cost of procedures, hospitalization, office visits, and prescription drugs. Similarly, providers will need better information at the time when services are provided about how much the consumer should pay them and how much the health plan will cover.

Consumer-directed health plans (also known as high-deductible plans) are the most obvious example of where more information is needed. In these plans, the consumer does not pay a co-payment at the beginning of a new year. Instead, he is responsible for the full cost of his care (except for an annual routine physical exam) up to a certain dollar amount—his deductible. As the system is set up now, the patient with a sore throat goes to the doctor and incurs a charge of, say, one hundred dollars. The doctor's office can see that the patient has Health Plan X but has no idea how much of the one-hundred-dollar office visit will be covered by the health plan. All of the key information about the patient's benefit plan and whether he has reached his deductible (in which case the health plan coverage would kick in) exists in the health plan's core benefits administration silo. Although the patient can request a periodic statement from the health plan telling him how much he has paid out of pocket toward the deductible amount or he can look it up online, the doctor's office cannot. As a result, in many cases, the patient receives care and goes home without having paid a cent at the doctor's office. The doctor is then stuck with a job she never trained for and to which she certainly never aspired—that of payment collector. Also, because information about how much money the patient is supposed to pay is not shared with the doctor's office, more paperwork is generated, consumer debt increases, and the doctor accumulates large amounts of accounts receivable, making it difficult to keep up with ongoing operating expenses.

Access to "real" cost information is extremely important to most consumers who are responsible for paying for the total cost of their care before reaching their deductible and then for paying a portion thereafter. Currently, their situation is analogous to going to a restaurant, having only a limited amount of money, and ordering from the menu without knowing how much each item costs. Again, the information about price exists in the healthcare system, but it is not available to the consumer, who has to decide how to spend a finite amount of money. It is hard to think of any other industry in which this model would be acceptable, except for meal plans in college cafeterias. Can you imagine going to a Nordstrom® store, selecting a pair of shoes without seeing the price, paying the sales clerk fifteen dollars, and then asking the store to let you know the full price when it bills you for the balance at the end of the month? Even if you have a health plan that uses co-payments and you know that the balance of the full cost of care will be covered, it is easy to see that information silos that outline costs contribute to the inefficiency of the healthcare system. The good news is that because most of the information that constituents lack is already captured elsewhere in the system, the problem of information silos can most definitely be solved, given adequate financial and information system design resources. By knitting together these information silos and enabling information to be available to constituents across the healthcare system, we can create the same transparency that operates in the retail world. Before we can create this convergence, however, we must confront a series of barriers in the way dollars flow through the healthcare system. In chapter 7, we will examine these barriers.

The inefficiency of our healthcare system is caused not only by the problem of fragmented information silos but also by the way financial interactions are set up. In chapter 7, we will examine how financial interactions affect the cost of healthcare and we will set up a zero-sum game among constituents.

Chapter 7

Follow the Dollar

Insanity: doing the same thing over and over again and expecting different results.

—Attributed to Albert Einstein

Everyone knows that enormous sums of money are spent on health-care in the United States each year. On that point, there seems to be almost no argument. Likewise, most people perceive the value we as a nation get for the total number of dollars spent on care to be inadequate. This dissatisfaction is most often discussed in the context of healthcare spending as a percentage of gross domestic product (GDP). Healthcare accounts for more than 17 percent of the GDP in the United States,[1] which—for a relatively wealthy nation—makes us a big outlier because this percentage is so high compared to other developed countries.

It is at this point that the thinking of intelligent leaders throughout our country diverges as industry experts and pundits wrestle with three repetitive themes that take turns on the front pages of prominent publications. First is the perplexing problem that we spend more than anybody else, yet we still have roughly fifty million people without health insurance. Second is that because healthcare costs employers so much money, companies build these higher costs into the goods they sell; thus, the relatively higher cost of healthcare coverage for our workers causes US companies to lose their edge in pricing products for an increasingly competitive world market. And third are the statistics I shared with you in chapter 1, whereby the United

States posts poorer scores on infant mortality and longevity than do many other developed nations. These are likely all familiar themes to you.

As this is not a book about healthcare economics or healthcare policy, spending a chapter analyzing these points doesn't really help us get to the solution. If we work under the assumption that we want every person in the country to have access to high-quality healthcare at an affordable cost, it's probably best to take a step back from the problem and examine it systematically, and once again think about drawing on experience from other industries where appropriate. In my experience, because so few people who are trying to solve the problem have a comprehensive understanding of the healthcare elephant, we can move from venue to venue of "experts" and quickly realize that there is no common view of the problem, even if the words sound similar. And if we listen carefully, there is always at least the faint murmur (more often the thunderous roar) of the almighty dollar driving the dialogue and behavior of the group participants, whether as an objective or as a necessity.

Understanding the Basic Dollar Flow

Until you understand at least the basics of how dollars flow through the healthcare system, it is difficult to comprehend fully why it works the way it does. So let's follow the dollar through the healthcare jungle and see where it goes. Returning to the supply-chain concept from chapter 4, we begin with the fact that in order to have an affordable system, we need to combine the demand for healthcare as well as the suppliers of healthcare into a predefined benefits package at a predictable price. Typically, the pricing for this benefit plan comes in the form of an insurance premium, and generally a benefit plan is classified as being either high deductible or low deductible. Once the deductible (the amount for which the consumer is responsible before the benefit plan starts paying) is reached, a predictable pattern of dollar distribution begins. This limited number of dollars must somehow be allocated among all of the parts of the system. Because the healthcare industry has never been designed so that the parts work together systematically toward a common objective, it is not surprising that each part of the system—pharmacies, hospitals, doctors, and suppliers—would vie for a greater proportion of each healthcare dollar. This zero-sum-game behavior is a natural result of competition and constrained resources.

What we must understand about all zero-sum games, however, is that if one "player" wins additional dollars within a constrained system, then the other players must collectively lose that same sum. Since as a nation we can't afford to spend more money on an ongoing basis, there are a great many constituents who are going to have to get less—or accomplish more for the same amount. What's important is that this allocation of resources be accomplished systematically and in ways that also improve healthcare value. I will lay out this methodology in chapter 8. For now, let's continue understanding the current dollar flow.

The Payer Pie: How Your Insurance Works

It is probably most useful to begin with the perspective of the payer, since the bulk of dollars are collected and distributed by the payer. If you are one of the more than two hundred million Americans covered by a private health plan, your health insurance company collects premiums from your employer or from you directly in order to administer your benefits. The illustration below shows how each premium dollar is distributed today.[2]

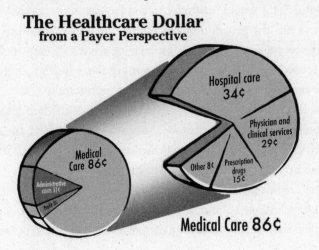

The Healthcare Dollar
from a Payer Perspective

Hospital care
34¢

Physician and clinical services
29¢

Other 8¢

Prescription drugs
15¢

Medical Care 86¢

Administrative costs 11¢

Profit 3¢

Medical Care 86¢

Approximately 11 percent of each premium dollar is used to administer your health benefits. This amount pays for all the typical business processes: designing your benefit plan; negotiating pricing contracts with hospitals, physicians, diagnostic centers, pharmacies, and other suppliers; enrolling you in the plan and collecting your premiums; processing and paying submitted claims; delivering customer service to consumers, employers, providers, and brokers; implementing care management guidelines for health plan members; and accounting for all these activities in order to remain solvent and able to price next year's benefit plans properly.

Let me make several observations that may not be obvious to the average consumer and that might put into context the highly charged topic of whether health plans garner excessive profit at your expense. First, in many parts of the country, up to half of the 11 percent may go to pay brokers for distributing the benefit plan product. Health plans typically have very small sales organizations and rely on brokers to work with employer groups and individuals who are considering purchasing health insurance. Second, health plans do not charge a markup on the claims they pay (represented by the 86 percent part of the pie). In fact, they nearly always pay a discounted price that has been prenegotiated. And by the way, when you are in your deductible phase (the amount you must pay before your health plan begins to cover your care) or when you are paying out of pocket, you benefit from these discounted prices. If your health plan had not negotiated these discounted prices, your out-of-pocket costs would be much higher. This would be similar to you paying the prices that Walmart's suppliers would charge you if Walmart had not already negotiated the discounted prices we see in the stores. Just imagine how much that would cost for the goods you buy at Walmart, and then think about how much the services that were not prenegotiated would cost in our healthcare system.

Now, let's further consider the 86 percent of the healthcare dollar pie that is paid directly by the health plan for the provision of medical care. It should be easy to understand why, in most cases, the doctors, hospitals, diagnostic centers, pharmacies, and suppliers are not thrilled with what they are getting paid. They are not thrilled for at least two reasons in addition to the negotiated pricing mentioned above. The first is that they don't particularly appreciate the fact that "their" patients or customers also happen to be members of a health plan and that when it comes to establishing and maintaining relationships with patients, these providers have to contend with a series of powerful third-party forces that have the ability to direct patients to certain doctors who have agreed to be part of the health plan's network and have accepted its reimbursement schedule. For example, my wife recently injured her knee and needed surgery. The knee surgeon she would have preferred was at loggerheads with our health plan and was not part of the provider network at that time. As a result, my wife went to another surgeon who was part of our health plan's network. The second reason these providers and suppliers are not too happy is that in order to receive payment, providers must comply with a series of required data and information submissions and follow certain care guidelines. As a result, in some cases, they feel that health plans are interfering with their ability to practice medicine the way they think is best. Both concerns have merit, and from a systems perspective, some friction between health plans and doctors is necessary to ensure that guidelines are thought through and implemented carefully. As I mentioned in chapter 4, not all treatments that physicians want to pursue are evidence based, nor are all less invasive approaches necessarily the right treatment for every patient.

Some physicians have sought to avoid this friction by attempting to circumvent health plans entirely in their patient relationships. I happen to live near an area where some established physicians refuse to accept the negotiated prices of leading health plans. These confident physicians believe that their patients will choose to see them even if the doctors do not agree to be in the health plan's network. They assume that their patients are both willing and able to pay a higher fee than they would if the health plan had negotiated a discount. This is a brilliant solution for physicians who exclusively serve the wealthiest 2 percent of Americans. However, it would not work for most doctors, whose patients need the help of health plans to negotiate discounts for them in order to keep healthcare affordable. Nor is this practical from a systems perspective; if this methodology were applied to the broader population (98 percent of Americans), most physician practices would spend significant financial and human resources chasing down payments from patients who could not afford this full-priced care. These resources could be better allocated to providing care.

The Value of Your Insurance Premium

To continue our explanation of the payer pie, the smallest slice of the pie, approximately 3 percent, is labeled as profit. Without getting into the complex details of pre-tax or after-tax profitability, the point is straightforward. Private health plans expect to earn a profit for being organizers of your healthcare supply chain and delivering what they believe is a solid benefit plan product at a reasonable price. They believe they deliver at least four kinds of value, which entitles them to earn a return on your premium dollar.

First, they offer you *pricing value*. As an individual, you would not be able to negotiate the same discounted rates that health plans negotiate on your behalf, just as you don't have Walmart's negotiating clout. Second, they offer you *access value* through an organized provider network so you do not have to Yellow Page your way through the healthcare system to find primary care doctors and specialists. Through their pre-established arrangements, health plans also support you in more smoothly accessing hospitals, diagnostic centers, and pharmacies within your health plan network. Third, they offer *insurance value*, which helps you by limiting your financial risk and providing a backstop against personal financial disaster that might result from a catastrophic accident or serious illness. Fourth, they offer *information value* by giving you information to help you make informed decisions about your benefits and care. This information comes in the form of printed and online information that explains your benefit plan, your provider network, and the rules you must follow in order to be sure your healthcare is covered. Health plans also offer an additional analytical type of information value rarely perceived by healthcare consumers: Health plans have the ability to review your health history and health risk assessment data, which enables them to take steps that might prevent you from developing more serious conditions. For example, by culling through data, your health plan can alert your physician if you forget to schedule an important preventive screening test.

Based on my experience, these four types of value are generally not fully appreciated by virtually anyone except health plan executives, knowledgeable benefits managers, and those who analyze and invest in health plan stocks. In my opinion, that is because most people don't want to hear or acknowledge the complexity involved in constructing an organized system of benefits and care. Most people don't want to hear how Walmart or FedEx work, either; they just want great products at low prices, as well as on-time delivery. Although people may not want the details, they do understand that a massive infrastructure is required to run these well-known retail enterprises. However, few people think about what it takes to run health-care organizations such as Blue Cross Blue Shield affiliates, Aetna, CIGNA, United Health Group, Humana, and Kaiser Permanente®.

"For-Profit" and "Not-for-Profit": Both Require More Dollars in Than Out

As we follow the dollar through the healthcare system, we must clear up one common misconception. People talk about various parts of the healthcare system as being "for-profit" or "not-for-profit," implying that the former is more apt to contribute to rising healthcare costs than the latter. Listen carefully to casual healthcare conversations. What you may hear is the general assumption that "for-profit" includes most health plans, hospitals that are not religiously affiliated, pharmacies, pharmaceutical companies, medical device manufacturers, and some types of doctors such as surgeons and radiologists. On the other hand, people assume that religiously affiliated hospitals, most doctors, Medicare, Medicaid, and a few health plans make up the "not-for-profit" category. The implication is that the for-profit entities somehow increase costs in the healthcare system, while not-for-profits are neutral at worst.

This assumption is erroneous; whether a particular entity is for-profit or not-for-profit, it has to bring in more money than it spends, or else it will not survive. This is known as an operating margin. In health plans and hospitals alike, the difference in day-to-day operating discipline is virtually undetectable among for-profits and their not-for profit counterparts. Not-for-profits enjoy benefits stemming from federal and state tax exemptions, and they access capital differently than for-profit entities do (particularly in contrast to publicly traded for-profit entities). However, the differences get quite technical in terms of financial reporting and capital raising. Both for-profits and not-for-profits are subject to regulatory oversight that, among other things, requires the establishment of reserves so that financial health can be maintained and easily measured and monitored. Not-for-profits must still charge enough to make a profit, but much of that profit is then reinvested in maintenance, infrastructure improvement, and reserves. For-profits invest in maintenance, infrastructure, and reserves as well, but they must also pay dividends or create an alternative type of financial return for investors. The bottom line is that whether hospitals or health plans are for-profit or not-for-profit, they are all motivated to make money.

Doctors Are For-Profit

One of the important points in understanding the flow of dollars through the system is that in the United States, doctors—just like many other parts of the healthcare system—are for-profit. Given the enormous cost of medical school and the resulting loans, combined with significant operating expenses such as office rent, equipment costs, administrative and nursing staff payroll, and medical malpractice insurance expenses, doctors in private practice must charge enough to cover their costs and, they hope, end up with sufficient income to live a lifestyle commensurate with the amount of time, effort, and money they have invested in their careers. And while many doctors currently choose to practice as salaried employees in a number of organizations, these organizations must cover the same types of costs and overhead.

And just how do you value the time, effort, and experience of a physician? As I mentioned earlier, it's pretty difficult to negotiate value when you are lying naked beneath a paper gown, worried about your impending diagnosis. As consumers, we get assistance in this regard from academic medical programs that establish selection mechanisms for medical school graduates to pursue different types of residencies in general and to specialize in specific types of medicine. Medical schools, academic medical centers, and teaching hospitals work together to rigorously evaluate candidates as well as the institution's teaching capability, essentially driving a self-regulated supply-and-demand matching system within the medical profession. Other than the tendency of the system to undervalue the general practitioner or primary care physician—and the enormous cost burden thrust upon most medical school students—it works pretty well. The entire area of pricing and reimbursement flows from this classification of generalists and specialists. Health plans take their cue from the physician community itself in terms of the relative value of services provided by different types of doctors. Let's look at the healthcare pie from the perspective of the physician.

How Providers See the Healthcare Pie

Physicians viewing the health plan distribution pie shown earlier might agree with it intellectually but would probably start turning red and possibly require medical assistance themselves if you were to say that only 11 percent of the healthcare dollar is spent on administration. For them, the notion that 86 percent of the dollar is reimbursement for medical care is a fallacy. That is because out of that 86 percent, hospitals, diagnostic centers, physicians, pharmacies, and other suppliers have administrative costs of their own for which they must use a portion of this "medical care" slice. They have to verify eligibility, submit claims, argue with the insurance company when services aren't authorized or claims aren't paid the way they believe they should be, figure out what the patient owes, send out statements and chase down collections from patients, and maintain proper credentials to be eligible for reimbursement. And by the way, running a business was not part of their medical school training, so there are numerous entities that assist physicians by doing some or all of these functions in exchange for a percentage of the medical billings. Doctors also need to pursue continuing professional education, build practices, and adapt to changing expectations of patients and health plans regarding how accessible doctors should be by telephone and online. Many find that by forming groups or by becoming employees of an integrated delivery system or hospital, they can spend more time practicing medicine.

Hospitals, despite generally having both professional management and the scale to deal with the administrative issues, also find it challenging to be reimbursed properly by health plans and consumers. Both hospitals and physicians struggle to keep track of patients. For example, their information systems were not originally designed to keep track of people using the unique numbering systems that insurance companies require—systems that ensure that the health plan doesn't count the same patient more than once just because his name is listed as "Jeffrey H. Margolis" for one transaction and "Jeff Margolis" for another. Although hospitals face challenges in this regard, being able to track patients in a manner compatible with the systems used by health plans is fundamental to being able to treat patients and collect reimbursement. Moreover, for both doctors and hospitals, the imperative that they invest heavily to implement electronic health records, or eventually be penalized if they do not, further adds to the perception of administrative burden.

Let the Games Begin

As you can imagine, both doctors and hospitals want to be reimbursed for their relative value to the healthcare supply chain in a manner they see as appropriate. Similarly, health plans want to price and pay for these same services in a manner they see as appropriate. Another chess piece on the board is how services provided to Medicare and Medicaid patients are reimbursed by the government. As mentioned in chapter 4, these amounts generally are not negotiable, and usually they are less than a private health plan will pay a physician or hospital. Therefore, if a hospital or doctor's practice treats a large number of Medicare or Medicaid patients, that facility has to recoup enough from private patient reimbursement to cover shortfalls from the government in order to have a positive operating margin. And so, the basic setup for the reimbursement game is that health plans negotiate with hospitals, doctors, pharmacies, and suppliers to establish prices for their eligible health plan members (the patients and customers of these constituents). Nearly all negotiations are done based upon a series of codes, most of which are indecipherable to the average healthcare consumer.

There are codes for diagnoses, codes for procedures or time spent during office visits, codes for diagnostic tests, codes for drug therapies, and so forth.

It's not important that you know all the codes. What is important is that you understand what behaviors are driven by the current system. In chapter 4, we talked about how the cost of healthcare is equal to the number of units multiplied by the price per unit. Well, there are many thousands of types of units. Some are very small and discrete, such as a common blood test, and some are very large, such as a heart transplant. If a particular service is assigned a low unit cost, some providers might be encouraged to pursue an increased number of these units in order to cover costs and achieve a desired level of income. This arrangement can set up a cat-and-mouse game in which providers might try to substitute more expensive services, or it can lead to behaviors that are unfortunate for patients and doctors, such as the all too familiar ten-minute office visit in which your doctor runs frantically from one exam room to the next so she can see enough patients to pay the rent. Wouldn't it be better if your doctor could be reimbursed for spending time with you to explain your diagnosis and possible treatment options?

Another place where inefficiency is rewarded by the system is in the area of medical technology. When new technology enters the marketplace, there is often a rush to use it. State-of-the-art imaging centers and other facilities are built to house the technology, and hospitals also invest in the new equipment. Because providers now need to pay for the expensive equipment, it is natural that they would tend to use it more (as discussed in chapter 4). They cannot pay for this equipment by charging higher prices for each test because health plans have already negotiated that pricing (and the government has fixed its pricing), so many providers turn to the only other possible way to recover their investment and stay solvent: they increase the volume (the number of units) of testing. Again, the incentives of the healthcare system—not ill will or malice—drive the ordering of expensive and often unnecessary testing. In most cases, this extra testing does not harm patients. But it significantly drives up the cost of healthcare.

Paying for Value versus Volume

Paying for units produced also has consequences (albeit unintentional) in places such as hospitals, where the sicker a patient gets, the more money the hospital makes. While no one wishes to harm patients, providers often have no incentive to use evidence-based medicine guidelines or to follow best practices, which would reduce the variation in care that so often leads to complications. Many health plans do have guidelines for the number of days a patient should spend in the hospital for a particular procedure, but if an infection develops or another complication arises, all bets are off.

About two years ago, my administrative assistant's husband went to the hospital for a planned hip surgery. The surgery went well, in a mechanical sense, and he was out of the hospital and walking in a matter of days. Following the surgery, he developed symptoms from a serious medication-resistant infection he had acquired at the hospital, and he was forced to return to the hospital for a several-week stay to fight the infection. This hospitalization was followed by several weeks of home-based drug therapy that prevented him from returning to work. The hospital staff and doctors likely had the best of intentions as they cared for my assistant's husband; however, as he got sicker, the hospital performed more tests to figure out the cause of his symptoms and to monitor his progress, and it billed more hospital days. While the hospital did not intentionally cause the infection, neither did it take enough precautions to prevent it. And while the health plan limits the number of days for which it will reimburse a hospital when a patient receives a hip replacement, in this case, the infection did not count against that limit. In the end, the hospital made far more money than it would have if the surgery had gone as planned.

Even under the best of circumstances, when all the right protocols are followed, people can have bad outcomes. But our current reimbursement structure that pays for the volume of care delivered increases the likelihood that situations like the one I just described will occur because there is little risk (and even a perverse incentive of sorts) in performing more tests and administering more treatment. If the hospital had known in advance that it would be paid only for the original planned hospital stay and hip replacement procedure, it would have been more likely to follow evidence-based medicine guidelines that might have prevented the infection.

What if we paid doctors and hospitals only for the procedures they were supposed to perform in the first place and not for the care that resulted from medical error? Would my assistant's husband's hospital have taken the extra precautions necessary to reduce or eliminate the probability of acquiring a secondary infection? Better yet, what would this man's outcome have been if the financial incentives had been designed to *reward* the hospital for following these protocols and for the *quality* of his care rather than for how many procedures were performed? The terrible irony is that in spite of the higher cost of his surgery and associated tests and procedures, my assistant's husband had a worse outcome than he would have had if fewer dollars had been spent on the right things. And in fairness to the hospital in this story, is it possible that the negotiated unit cost for the hip surgery might negatively have affected the hospital's ability to invest in precautions that might have led to a better outcome while still making a fair profit? If the health plan had collaborated with the hospital to understand the true costs of providing high-quality care that would lead to a better outcome for more of its hip replacement patients (including investment in infection-reduction programs), then the plan might have agreed to a slightly higher reimbursement, which in turn could have resulted in a lower total cost for the hip replacement and, therefore, higher value. Volume-driven medicine isn't much fun for anybody, and that is why unit pricing as a primary reimbursement methodology in many situations is probably not the best idea we can come up with. At the very least, we need to ask these questions and try to develop incentives that will encourage the best results.

In fact, there are other types of reimbursement that are not based on volume and are already in use today, including *capitation*, *episodes of care*, *bundled payments*, and *per diem* arrangements. In one type of *capitation* arrangement, a physician or physician group is paid a flat fee per patient per month and is responsible for delivering all of each patient's nonhospital care within that budgeted amount. Another payment arrangement is *episodes of care*, in which a physician, hospital, or both in combination are paid one total price for the treatment of a single condition over a specific length of time. An example of an episode of care might be when the obstetrician-gynecologist and hospital are paid a flat rate for a patient's prenatal care from the beginning of the first trimester through hospital discharge for a normal pregnancy and birth. *Bundled payments* relate to the hip replacement example in that the doctor and hospital would be paid one price for all preparations and care related to that procedure. The care would be under warranty, so the doctor and hospital would have to figure out how to pay for treatment whether it goes smoothly or involves unanticipated care due to complications. Another form of reimbursement is known as *per diem*, whereby a flat fee is paid for a certain level of daily care in a hospital or skilled nursing facility.

There are a variety of other methods of reimbursement beyond the ones just described. What you really need to understand is that in today's healthcare system, where so much more importance is placed on unit costs than on the quality or outcome of what those units produce, merely shifting where in the healthcare system the dollars are spent is much like moving the deck chairs around on the *Titanic*. Nothing will systematically change. In contrast, reimbursement methods that are not based on volume (such as those just described) can help promote systematic change.

Furthermore, if you as a consumer do not understand what these prices are for the relative value you are going to receive, you will have trouble making sound, well-informed decisions. We need a better kind of pricing in healthcare, and it must be transparent so that it's not just a secret between the health plan and the doctor, the health plan and the hospital, or the health plan and the pharmacy.

Getting Blame Out of the Way

Are you beginning to see why the average consumer could never navigate the healthcare jungle alone? Do you also understand why so many of the problems in our healthcare system have far less to do with the greed of health plans or doctors and much more to do with how the system perpetuates and rewards inefficiency?

In contrast to healthcare, the farming industry provides a good example of how information about best practices, technology, and incentives can be used to improve efficiency. Can you imagine if farmers, seed companies, farming- and irrigation-equipment manufacturers, and fertilizer producers spent their energy fighting with one another in pursuit of a limited dollar pool? Rather than producing enough food to feed much of the world, as the United States does today, we might be wondering why so large a percentage of GDP is committed to agriculture while a disproportionate percentage of our citizens is starving. Instead, farmers and others have focused their energy on continuously improving the quality and productivity of every element in the agricultural supply chain. As a result, they succeeded in driving the yield per acre to levels that were science fiction several decades ago.

My wife's family comes from a fertile farming region of Nebraska, so I have heard the farmers at the local coffee shop complain about the government, the mega-farming corporations, the unfair business practices of the so-and-so's in the next town, and the inevitable decline of life as they knew it. Yet I have also seen these same farmers embrace information technology in the small family farm to increase crop yields while minimizing use of water and depletion of arable land, to maintain equipment according to specifications that lower the total cost of ownership over the equipment's useful life, and to use other best practices while adding personal experience and hunches. At the end of the day, the complaining is cultural but not consumptive; everybody knows the crop yield produced for a dollar this year is just not going to be good enough next year. The fact that your family has farmed the land for one hundred years entitles you to nothing, which makes the incentive to improve the way the farm works very powerful. And the allure of applying new technologies, whether seeds, equipment, or chemicals, keeps the job intellectually stimulating—you are constantly learning. I have observed the same learning culture on family ranches in Wyoming and Colorado. The wide availability of the Internet has leveled the playing field for farmers and ranchers and for those who seek to supply them or distribute the goods they have produced.

In polar opposition to healthcare, the agricultural industry has developed the ability to produce so much high-quality product at such a low price (even as the number of farmers has precipitously declined) that in most years the government and the industry collaborate on the level of production necessary to keep prices from being too low, essentially ensuring that the cost to consumers keeps in step with general inflation targets. Yes, there are bad years when drought or disease drives unexpected increases in costs, and there are good years when bumper crops exceed planning expectations, but the world does not criticize the ability of the United States to feed itself (although it might deservedly criticize what we eat).

Stop Debating and Start Engineering

Constituents in the healthcare industry need to stop spending so much energy squaring off against one another in a zero-sum game. We need to acknowledge that we must increase healthcare "yield"—the amount of high-quality output we get for each dollar spent. We need to continuously apply our best economic discoveries at both the overall system level and the individual benefits level, in combination with our best scientific and integrated medical findings at the population and individual levels, to increase this "yield." Engineering healthcare to function more efficiently as a system is the only way to curb our healthcare spending and become able to cover the uninsured without increasing the cost of healthcare more than necessary.

In order for us to become a nation of winners in the healthcare game, we have to shift our attention from policy and payment allocation to the engineering and deliberate design that will make the healthcare system do more with less money. In chapter 8, we'll examine how to accomplish this by bridging from the current healthcare system to a better one.

Chapter 8

Integrated Healthcare Management:
The Solution

An invasion of armies can be resisted, but not an idea whose time has come.

—Victor Hugo, *The History of a Crime: Deposition of a Witness,*
1852, trans. 1877

It's easy to understand why many people are pessimistic about whether we can fix the US healthcare system. As we have seen, healthcare is huge and complex. And rather than being intentionally designed as an effective system, it has evolved into a chaotic jungle. As a result, we have poor communication among constituents, fragmented information for you and your doctor to use in making important decisions, and misaligned incentives that perpetuate unhealthful behaviors in consumers and unnecessary practice variation among providers. These flaws have contributed to today's soaring healthcare costs. To make matters worse, the lack of an overall systematic design often causes constituents to work against one another, even while total healthcare spending in the United States continues to outpace overall economic growth. But as history has repeatedly shown, it is precisely in times of crisis that some of the best innovations are born, and healthcare is no exception. We can transform the US healthcare system if we take a systems approach. The key to the solution is Integrated Healthcare Management (IHM).

Integrated Healthcare Management: Sustainable Affordability and Quality

Integrated Healthcare Management is an approach that addresses the affordability crisis while systematically improving the quality of healthcare. It uses systematic design and information technology to share information and to align incentives among healthcare constituents so they can make better choices that result in more effective care. IHM combines the best processes and knowledge we have for designing and administering healthcare benefits, the best processes and knowledge in care management, and information about the specific preferences and personal values of each constituent to create benefit plans, incentives, and information tools tailored to each individual using the system. To be clear, we can implement the IHM approach even amid any uncertainty over whether the Patient Protection and Affordable Care Act, passed in 2010, remains fully intact.

By connecting the data contained in the silos we discussed in chapter 6 (core benefits administration, care management, and constituent information), and by developing incentives throughout the healthcare system that promote better health instead of simply providing more care, IHM will create opportunities for consumers to become more informed, active participants in their own healthcare. With complete, up-to-date information clearly presented during every interaction with the healthcare system, consumers will be better equipped to make important healthcare choices in partnership with their providers. If you look at the diagram on page 141, you will see how IHM can use information technology to make the primary groups of information in the healthcare system connect. This area of convergence is what I call the "IHM Convergence Zone." It is where information will be shared in formats that each constituent will find helpful. I will describe some examples later in this chapter. This IHM Convergence Zone is also where incentives that promote better health results at a lower cost can be developed to encourage consumers, providers, employers, and brokers to work together toward the same goals.

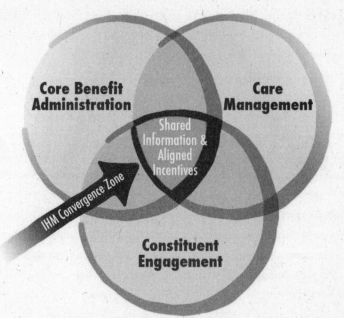

IHM will deliver better healthcare at lower cost by focusing on three main objectives:

- **To inform the personal choices** we as consumers make about our healthcare benefit and treatment decisions as well as our behavior. These informed decisions will result in greater consumer satisfaction and expanded access to the care and services we need the most in order to maintain and improve our health.
- **To reduce unwarranted variation in care** and excessive medical testing and procedures through adherence to peer-reviewed evidence-based medicine guidelines while also ensuring that appropriate care is not overlooked or withheld. The result will be lower medical costs and higher-quality care and patient safety.
- **To engineer administrative inefficiencies out of the system** so that improved administrative efficiency will result in administrative simplification, saving both consumers and providers time while also reducing hassles.

IHM is an especially powerful approach for several reasons. First, benefit plans will be tailored to meet the individual health needs of each consumer, as opposed to today's one-size-fits-all approach in which the benefits covered and the level at which they are covered have little to do with the health status and demographics of each consumer. Second, healthcare information technology will knit together data about benefits coverage, treatment choices, costs, funding mechanisms (like healthcare savings accounts or available government subsidies), and quality. Because information will no longer be locked up in silos, constituents—especially providers and consumers—will be able to collaborate more about healthcare decisions, and the huge knowledge gap between what patients and doctors each understand about treatment choices will shrink. Information will be personalized, taking into account each patient's health status, age and life stage, economic status, personal values, and personal preferences; this personalization, as we saw earlier, can increase the likelihood that a patient will follow a doctor's instructions. Finally, IHM will enable the development of incentives that are aligned among constituents. These incentives will reward behaviors that promote the attainment of each patient's individual health goals and will discourage unwarranted variations in medical practice across the system. Because it is systematic, scalable (able to be used for large numbers of people), and repeatable, IHM is not simply a bandage, but a prescription for a sustainable solution.

IHM can be activated through a systematic, well-designed application of information technology that enables clear and relevant information to reach constituents where they need it, when they need it, and in the format they will find helpful for each situation. There are four key elements of Integrated Healthcare Management: evidence-based medicine guidelines, aligned economic incentives (such as value-based benefits and value-based provider reimbursement), systematic health management, and active communication among constituents within a culture of health.

1. Evidence-Based Medicine Guidelines

Evidence-based medicine (EBM) guidelines (also called "best practices" or "evidence-based guidelines") form the foundation upon which IHM sits.

As I mentioned earlier in this book, these treatments have been shown by peer-reviewed scientific research to be comparatively more effective than other methods. There is a large and growing body of clinical research results (i.e., evidence) from which standards for effective care are developed and new incentives can be created. Evidence-based medicine guidelines come from a variety of settings, including research universities and academic medical centers, not-for-profit healthcare foundations, and for-profit health research and clinical trial organizations that gather and package evidence-based findings into systematic guidelines. EBM guidelines can range from relatively straightforward (seemingly common sense) to extremely complex guidelines based on a person's unique genetic makeup and body chemistry. As knowledge of the effectiveness of one treatment compared to another continues to grow, the body of EBM guidelines also grows and is constantly updated. One relatively simple example is the recommendation I mentioned earlier in chapter 6 that diabetic patients should receive annual eye exams to screen for an eye disease that could cause blindness. Another example is the guideline that following a heart attack, patients should be given beta-blockers to reduce the risk of another heart attack. Other evidence-based guidelines can easily be followed directly by patients and can yield some powerful health improvements. Some examples are to follow the guidelines for recommended daily exercise and nutrition issued by the US Department of Health and Human Services and to have regular mammograms and other screening tests that are recommended based on your age, health status, and risk factors.

When evidence-based medicine guidelines are followed by providers and consumers, better care is provided at a lower cost because unnecessary and ineffective care is reduced and healthy behaviors are encouraged. Let's take low back pain as an example. Studies show that patients who participate in a physical therapy and weight loss regimen have a similar rate of positive outcomes compared to patients who have back surgery.[1] Back surgery costs far more and, like any surgery, can put the patient at greater risk for complications. Yet many patients opt for surgery, in part because their doctors recommend it and also because patients—and in many cases, doctors—do not have up-to-date information on the outcomes of various treatment options.

As I can personally attest, the decision to have surgery can sometimes lead to more care due to unexpected complications. Keep in mind that the low back pain example is only one of many that show how lack of information about evidence-based medicine can lead to expensive decisions and questionable outcomes. In my own case, following seven surgeries, three of which were performed to correct complications or errors from prior surgeries, my doctors and I learned that my strict adherence to a specific regimen of medication, diet, and exercise is the major determining factor in keeping me out of the emergency room and preventing additional expensive medical procedures. The IHM approach ensures that providers and consumers have relevant information about evidence-based medicine before important, costly decisions are made. From both a quality and cost (not to mention human) perspective, patients should not have to endure unnecessary pain and inconvenience without first actively pursuing less invasive measures that have been shown to yield an equal or better result, often at a lower cost.

2. Aligned Economic Incentives: Value-Based Benefits and Value-Based Provider Reimbursement

As we have seen in previous chapters, there is no systematic mechanism designed into today's healthcare system to align the behavior of patients and providers toward a common goal. IHM uses information technology and redefined incentives to encourage partnership between patient and provider in achieving the patient's health goals.

> ### Value-Based Benefits
>
> Value-based benefits remove barriers for preventive and effective patient care and provide incentives and rewards to the consumer for making the right choices, while discouraging care that is proven ineffective or dangerous.

How do your actions as a healthcare consumer affect your own cost of healthcare? This is an important question, but if you have health insurance already, you might not think your own behavior really matters because much of the care you may need as the result of poor decisions will be covered anyhow. However, while in the short term most of your care may be covered, over time your choices could affect not only your out-of-pocket costs, but also your overall health status. It's not just big choices (as in the low back pain surgery example) that affect the cost of healthcare, but everyday decisions as well. How much you exercise; what you eat for breakfast, lunch, and dinner; and whether you smoke all can affect your likelihood of developing serious and costly diseases such as type 2 diabetes and heart disease. Even daily hygiene habits can affect your susceptibility to a range of serious ailments.

However, in today's system there is often little connection between the choices consumers make and how much they pay for healthcare. Also, most benefit plans today do not systematically target specific health goals for each consumer, and you have few financial incentives to engage in behaviors that keep you healthy, prevent the onset of disease, and encourage you to manage diseases you may already have. In today's system, your insurance premium amount typically is the same whether you follow evidence-based guidelines for weight and exercise or spend your days on the couch eating doughnuts.

To help consumers more actively engage in their healthcare decisions, IHM applies *value-based benefits*—benefits designed to encourage consumers to make choices that have been shown scientifically to lead to healthier outcomes. Value-based benefits are so named because they have the potential to increase the value of each healthcare dollar by encouraging consumers to follow evidence-based medicine guidelines—the treatment shown to be comparatively most effective. In the world according to IHM, coverage will be customized according to each consumer's particular health profile, whether the consumer is healthy, suffers from severe chronic conditions, or falls somewhere in between. Consumers will receive a variety of financial incentives for making choices that move them closer to meeting specific healthcare goals and for engaging in behaviors that follow evidence-based medicine. Again, the purpose of this kind of benefit coverage is to make it easier for consumers to receive preventive and effective care, to provide incentives and rewards for progress, and to discourage choices that either could increase your risk for developing certain conditions or are not shown by evidence-based medicine to be the most effective treatments.

The connection between healthcare costs and behavior change is vital. When I traveled around speaking to nearly two thousand employees at our various offices, I asked the question, "Why don't you purposely drive your car into a tree?" It probably seemed like a ridiculous question because the answer seemed so obvious. However, the first answer I got most frequently was, "Because my car insurance premium would go up," followed by, "Because I could get hurt or killed." My employees' response could not have been more effective in making my point. Somehow, the auto insurance industry has taught consumers that even though you cannot avoid all accidents, there is a financial incentive for you to try. However, consumers have not made the equivalent connection regarding their behaviors and their health, in part because health insurance today gives us no financial incentives to follow evidence-based guidelines established to promote better health (such as adhering to a preventive drug regimen or following guidelines developed by the Department of Health and Human Services for how much exercise per week is recommended to help prevent various diseases).

When a person with risk factors such as high cholesterol, high blood pressure, obesity, or any combination thereof opts not to follow the daily exercise recommended by his doctor, chooses fatty meats over lean meats or fruits and vegetables, and empties the salt shaker onto his food each night, he is figuratively driving his body into a tree. However, although he risks getting hurt, his behavior currently does not lead to any financial consequence. While it's a free country and people should have the right to choose their own behaviors, our nation would be well served from a systems science viewpoint if certain behaviors were associated with financial incentives designed to bring about the changes that would reduce waste and improve health. Equally important is that consumers be given the tools to understand the financial implications of each behavior and receive help keeping their bodies "on the road" if that is what they choose to do.

Value-based benefits are not a new concept but are just now becoming familiar to the average consumer. Many of our nation's largest employers are asking health plans to incorporate value-based benefits into the design of their benefit plans for employees in order to reduce costs while increasing adherence to evidence-based medicine. There are two types of value-based benefits: "carrots" and "sticks." The carrots are rewards in the form of low costs, discounts, cash, and other positive incentives for making decisions that follow guidelines for effective care, including preventive care, patient education programs, and healthy behaviors such as working out at the gym. These "carrots" also include health plans waiving co-pays for preventive drugs or therapies that, according to EBM, have been shown to help patients maintain a better health status and reduce costs. Some examples of this type of preventive care for which the co-pay might be waived are asthma inhalers, cholesterol-lowering drugs, or beta-blockers following a heart attack.

The "sticks" are financial penalties or higher costs for care that does not follow guidelines for evidence-based medicine. Value-based benefits give you choices, but there are different out-of-pocket price tags attached to each option. In the case of low back pain, you can choose from various treatment options, but choosing the surgery will cost you more (particularly if you don't attempt less invasive approaches first) because it has not been shown scientifically to be more effective than less expensive options.

Value-Based Provider Reimbursement

Value-based provider reimbursement supports and rewards for delivering effective care while discouraging ineffective/inefficient care.

Just as value-based benefits encourage responsibility for consumption (on the part of the consumer), value-based provider reimbursement encourages accountability for high-quality production (on the part of the provider). In the last chapter, we saw some examples of value-based provider reimbursement, including capitation, episodes of care, bundled payments, and per diem.

In general, value-based reimbursement rewards physicians for taking a broader, more active role in the management of patient health and pays them for results and quality instead of solely for specific visits or procedures. Because quality outcomes often are hard to define in healthcare, the best proxy is following evidence-based guidelines for care. As value-based reimbursement evolves, we will find better, more creative ways to ensure that physicians have the information they need to follow these guidelines. As evidence-based medicine continues to develop, so, too, will innovative ways to reimburse healthcare providers for value and quality, rather than for volume (the number of units of care they provide). Providers will be rewarded for delivering effective care in keeping with evidence-based medicine, and their compensation will be negatively affected if they do not follow evidence-based guidelines. As I mentioned earlier, some doctors' opinions of what constitutes the best care for their patients may differ from EBM guidelines. While such situations are relatively rare, processes already exist in the system for doctors to advocate for exceptions to be made on behalf of their patients. Integrated Healthcare Management and value-based provider reimbursement do not seek to end appropriate doctor discretion. There are some examples of value-based provider reimbursement already in the marketplace—one of which is normal pregnancy and delivery—where provider payment has moved from volume-based reimbursement (payment by unit of care) to value-based reimbursement for an entire episode of care. Under the value-based reimbursement system, the provider in this example is paid a set fee for all the components of care necessary for a patient's healthy pregnancy and delivery (including doctor visits, testing based on evidence-based guidelines, patient education about nutrition and other important topics, and delivery). The incentive for providing care is linked to the health and well-being of the patient throughout the pregnancy and to the doctor's adherence to procedural steps, not to how many times the doctor sees the patient. For example, in this case, the doctor's compensation allows—and even encourages—time for her to answer questions and educate her patients. Although this approach may seem obvious, it wasn't very many years ago that there were not even incentives in place to ensure that the cost of a normal pregnancy and delivery was predictable. Not only will IHM increase predictability for the cost of care, but it will also improve quality by ensuring that providers and patients both follow the steps that have the greatest potential for a healthy outcome. Moreover, IHM allows for the continuous evaluation and refinement of quality within the bundled reimbursement for a normal episode of care.

Returning to the example of my assistant's husband in chapter 7, under a value-based provider reimbursement system the hospital would be paid for the hip surgery as an episode of care, rather than for each test or procedure performed. Another important point about evidence-based provider reimbursement is that pricing for the intended procedure is under warranty by the hospital that performs it, and if any additional work were required, the provider would be financially responsible. Under a well-run system of value-based provider reimbursement, the price a health plan pays for an episode of care, such as a hip replacement, is prenegotiated based on the assumption that providers will follow evidence-based medicine throughout the course of treatment. Because the cost is fixed, there is great incentive for doctors and hospitals to ensure that all procedures that will reduce the chance of complications (such as infections) and that consequently will keep costs down are followed.

Value-based provider reimbursement also offers an opportunity for providers to be paid not only for delivering care according to evidence-based medicine guidelines but also for coordinating other care that patients need from specialists, home health aides, nutritionists, and other providers. Likewise, value-based provider reimbursement provides an opportunity to reimburse doctors for monitoring how their patients are progressing toward their health goals. In addition to the other examples of value-based provider reimbursement already discussed, there are many others already emerging.

The *patient-centered medical home* is not a place, as its name might suggest, but rather a model for delivering care. It is a team-based arrangement led by a primary care physician who takes on the role of a healthcare quarterback and is reimbursed for managing all of a patient's care. In certain cases in which patients have a chronic illness such as diabetes or cancer, specialists (such as endocrinologists or medical oncologists) are best suited to assume the role of healthcare quarterback. These doctors arrange primary and specialty care when necessary and, similar to the role of gatekeeper (as in the earlier managed care attempts discussed in chapter 4), they coordinate with other doctors on the patient's team and collaborate with their patients to ensure they are making progress on their treatment plans. If necessary, they also make sure their patients have home healthcare and other support services upon discharge from the hospital. Depending on the particular needs of each patient, the care team might include doctors, nurse practitioners, physician assistants, nurses, nutritionists, pharmacists, social workers, and educators. Patient-centered medical homes emphasize prevention, access to care when patients need it, and the use of technology and information to encourage communication.

Another example of value-based provider reimbursement is paying providers for episodes of care for acute specialty care such as heart surgery. This care is often provided at *centers of excellence*, which are designed for diagnosing and treating such conditions as cancer, women's health issues, orthopedics, diabetes, and heart and vascular disease. This model is relatively well known today. Under a value-based reimbursement model, these providers would be required to warranty their work. For example, a patient who had a hip replacement at an orthopedic center of excellence and later experienced complications would be readmitted up to six months out at no extra cost.

Other developing value-based delivery models include online *e-visits* and *telemedicine*, in which providers are reimbursed for the time they spend providing care via telephone, the Internet, or other modes of communication. A nascent example of value-based provider reimbursement includes paying physicians for the delivery of *patient education*. For example, doctors would be compensated for having patients watch a video, read a booklet, or go to a class in which they learn what to expect before and after a surgical procedure (such as a wisdom tooth extraction or joint replacement) or before undergoing treatment for an illness such as cancer. Paying providers for these types of information-sharing services will spawn dynamic new methods of coding and reimbursement. Currently, no specific procedural payment code exists for explaining the details of an illness or condition to a patient. Therefore, doctors have little incentive to spend extra time with you if you have questions—although, fortunately, many still do. More to the point, many doctors schedule follow-up office visits that consume patient time and often take place too far after the fact to be helpful.

There is general agreement in the healthcare industry that paying providers solely for volume (the number of units they produce) is not a good practice; however, there is less consensus about what is the best reimbursement alternative. One school of thought suggests that providers should be compensated for delivering successful outcomes, such as a hip replacement without infection or other complications. While I support this notion for certain procedures or episodes of care where the measurement of an outcome is obvious (such as a patient's ability to walk and have adequate range of motion after having knee replacement surgery), in many cases where the specific outcome is too narrowly defined, this approach might not lead to the highest overall health status for the patient. So sometimes the best application of value-based provider reimbursement is to ensure that a provider has followed the proper steps, rather than to pay the provider for a specific outcome. One example is the question of whether a doctor should be reimbursed if cholesterol levels for his entire population of patients improve, or whether the doctor should be paid for ensuring that all these patients undergo proper blood chemistry testing in which a variety of risk factors (not only cholesterol) could be analyzed and acted upon. The best solution to this problem may well be to pay doctors for ensuring that their entire population of patients follows evidence-based medicine guidelines for testing, rather than solely for the results of procedures.

Another argument for paying for adherence to evidence-based medicine guidelines rather than solely for outcomes is that while doctors have control over whether they follow certain steps, they cannot always control outcomes. To use an example I introduced earlier, in the case of a diabetic patient, the doctor should be paid for ensuring that her patients receive an annual eye exam (an evidence-based guideline), not for whether the patient does or does not develop a disease of the retina. The doctor cannot necessarily control whether the patient develops a disease, but she can make sure she takes evidence-based precautions against such an outcome. Even if providers follow every guideline to the letter, people can still get sicker or even die. Similarly, there are some cases where providers do not follow evidence-based medicine guidelines and rely instead on anecdotal evidence, and the patient ends up with a positive outcome nonetheless. From a perspective of systems design and continuous quality improvement, we are far better off encouraging providers to follow what we know to be the best guidelines available, even if they don't lead to positive outcomes 100 percent of the time. The alternative—paying providers to hit an outcome target without following best practices—is a far less certain proposition. Going back to chapter 3, "The Lexus and the Human," it is important to understand that although defects and problems are bound to occur even in a best-of-class process, they can be solved more quickly if the process in which they occur is repeatable and thus the impact of changing any single step in it can be analyzed. This is true in manufacturing, software development, and the practice of medicine.

Another caveat about value-based provider reimbursement (and IHM in general) is that it is not intended to penalize doctors in emergency rooms. When trauma cases and other situations requiring real emergency care burst through the ER doors, this is not the time for ER doctors to focus on how they will be reimbursed. Because they constantly must triage patients, emergency rooms tend to have very good standardized procedures. It is important to realize that although this type of care may be the most likely to make headlines and be featured on prime-time television, true emergency care accounts for only a small percentage of all of the care provided. IHM is designed to drive systematic improvement of the majority of nonemergency care because that is where there is the greatest potential to reduce cost and improve quality.

3. Systematic Health Management

In today's world, our healthcare system focuses on the management of a very small percentage of very sick people. In contrast, *systematic health management* is about proactively looking across populations of people—from the healthy to the chronically ill—to help healthy people stay healthy, sick people not get sicker, and patients along the entire spectrum improve their health status. Systematic health management includes identifying and segmenting people into groups according to their health needs, developing a health improvement plan or patient "itinerary" for each patient, and monitoring progress over time to ensure that patients meet their health goals.

Systematic health management will work most effectively if patients and providers (primary care physicians in particular) each have access to the patient's health improvement plan in a format that contains the level of information best suited to each of them. This plan will give a comprehensive view of the patient's healthcare needs and goals (including current and target measures for cholesterol, blood pressure, weight, and other important health indicators). The health improvement plan will encourage dialogue between doctor and patient about overall health status, prevention, and recommended treatment options if the patient becomes sick or injured. Ideally, the provider's version of the health improvement plan will be aligned with the patient's so that both doctor and patient will have coordinated incentives to move the patient toward improving and maintaining the patient's health. When doctors follow evidence-based medicine guidelines, they will be rewarded financially according to value-based provider reimbursements; similarly, patients will be rewarded via value-based benefits for making progress on their health improvement plans. Later in this chapter, Sarah's story provides specific examples of how IHM will help consumers and doctors manage health in a deliberate, systematic way.

4. Constituent Engagement within a "Culture of Health"

IHM will encourage all constituents—consumers, providers, employers, and brokers—to become engaged and active in improving and maintaining health. Rather than focusing mainly on care when people are sick or injured, our healthcare system will also provide incentives and support for choices that help healthy people maintain and improve their health. In other words, we will all be operating within a *culture of health,* rather than of illness. "Culture" is one of those words that everyone knows but that is difficult to define. One analogy for the term "culture of health" is to think about people's consciousness regarding water conservation. If you were out for a walk and you saw your neighbor's sprinkler system leaking water into the street, you would probably knock on his door for several reasons. First, you would recognize that water is a precious commodity that should not be wasted. Second, you would realize that the leak would cost your neighbor money he doesn't need to spend. A third reason for your knock on the door (perhaps a bit more sophisticated than your other reasons) is that you would realize your neighbor's waste of water might end up costing you and everyone else around you more money or result in a situation where you didn't have enough water. When we all start thinking about healthcare in a similar way, we will start to move toward a culture of health—one in which we realize that each of us plays a role in managing our own healthcare costs and improving our personal health to the greatest extent possible, while also taking responsibility for how our actions affect healthcare within the broader context of our communities and our nation.

As constituents work together within this culture of health, each of their roles and responsibilities will change.

The Constituents' Changing Roles

Consumers like you and me will take on greater personal responsibility, both for choosing the benefit plan that best meets our health needs within our financial constraints and for making good decisions when we need care. We will need to add healthcare to our list of budget items and learn about the various tools for saving for our healthcare expenses, as I will explain further in chapter 10.

Providers will assume broader responsibility for managing patient health, not just for the very sick but also for healthy patients. To this end, providers will develop their understanding of evidence-based medicine and recommend EBM treatment options as a means of avoiding unnecessary and ineffective care while improving the health of their patients. They will also help educate patients about wellness and prevention and recommend programs in areas such as exercise, weight management, nutrition, and smoking cessation.

Employers will help their employees to become more savvy as healthcare consumers and to learn how the decisions they make can lead to better health and lower costs. They will also promote workplace wellness, prevention, and safety and increase awareness in these areas.

Brokers will facilitate collaboration between the employer and the health plan to drive employees to develop behaviors that reflect healthier lifestyles.

Sarah's Story: IHM in Action

To understand how the key elements of IHM work, let's experience a day in the life of a typical consumer in the IHM world who we'll call "Sarah." Sarah is about to sign up for health coverage. She is a forty-year-old healthy professional who, like many of us, sometimes forgets to keep up to date with routine screenings (such as mammograms) and doesn't always make time to exercise. Sarah's daughter has difficulty keeping her asthma under control. Sarah's husband struggles with his weight and experiences low back pain. Although Sarah has noticed that the health benefits available through her employer have changed markedly over the past couple of years because of rising healthcare costs, she doesn't realize how her own personal choices affect those costs. Let's follow Sarah as she moves through each step in the life cycle and experiences the link between cost and healthy behavior in an IHM world.

Sarah's health plan guided
her to the right plan.

Selecting and Enrolling in a Benefits Plan

This year, Sarah's company's open enrollment period begins somewhat differently than in years past. Her company's benefits representative holds a meeting to explain the connection between personal choices and the cost of healthcare. He also describes a new plan that will reward Sarah and her family for making healthy choices in diet and exercise and for complying with directions from their doctors. He explains that the plan will be tailored to Sarah and her family's specific healthcare needs, with lower out-of-pocket payments for preventive care and other care they need to stay healthy in exchange for higher costs for elective procedures and care that is deemed "unnecessary."

Before Sarah enrolls, her health plan sends her a family health profile based on her family's previous interactions with the healthcare system and on information she has voluntarily provided (e.g., her preference to receive notifications via e-mail). The profile describes her family's health status and includes a personalized health improvement plan, or health "itinerary." This health itinerary includes information about each family member, his or her particular health concerns (such as her husband's being overweight according to established guidelines), the potential risks for not acting on these health concerns (such as the possibility that Sarah's husband could develop diabetes or coronary artery disease because he is overweight), and the financial incentives Sarah and her family will have in their new benefit plan to encourage healthy behaviors.

Sarah interacts with her plan in
new ways to optimize her health.

During the enrollment process, the health plan guides Sarah and her family toward a benefits plan that is tailored to her family's health needs. She learns that her plan encourages adherence to industry best practices (evidence-based medicine guidelines) for managing chronic diseases like asthma, and because her daughter has asthma, her plan includes 100 percent coverage for asthma-related prescriptions and services. It also includes 100 percent coverage for Sarah's yearly mammogram. Her employer's benefits plans in previous years did not completely pay for these services, so Sarah either paid out of pocket or tried to go a little longer without them.

Committing to health helped
Sarah's whole family save money.

Staying Healthy

In the past, Sarah didn't think about her health plan unless someone needed care or she had a question about her benefits. But the health improvement plan she committed to as part of her new benefits provides a mechanism for tracking progress toward her family's health goals on an ongoing basis, not just when they are sick. Best of all, her plan rewards her family when they make healthy choices or achieve key plan milestones. For example, if her husband completes his first month of a new exercise program at the local gym, he'll receive a fifty-dollar incentive. Also, from time to time, Sarah receives helpful reminders about ways that her family can save money. To Sarah's surprise, her monthly statement shows she is paying less in monthly premiums because she and her family are achieving their health goals.

Sarah's family has a health coach assigned to them by her health plan. The health coach has access to all the relevant information about Sarah's family's health status and provides support to Sarah and her family to help them stay on track with their health improvement plans. The health coach not only provides quick and relevant answers to Sarah's questions, but also suggests ways her family can save money. For example, if her daughter completes a patient education program on asthma management, Sarah can save money on co-payments for her daughter's office visits. Sarah also notices that her family's doctors have useful information they did not have in the past. At her daughter's last appointment, the doctor noticed that she was five days overdue for a refill of her asthma inhaler. Sarah was able to pick up a refill on the way home and also ask her daughter to warn her when the inhaler begins to run out.

Accessing Care

When Sarah's husband, Bill, needs treatment for his back pain, his experience is dramatically different than in the past. To begin with, his doctor has access to his electronic health record and his health improvement plan. During the consultation, his doctor reviews the treatment options with him, using an electronic tool that compares the cost and quality of those treatments. His options include seeing an orthopedic specialist for surgery or using pain medication and exercise to address the root cause of his back pain—his weight.

Bill agrees to continue with his weight loss plan because he sees that in his case, surgery is not recommended unless other, less invasive measures have been tried first. Bill also realizes that surgery would be expensive and that he would have to pay for a large part of the cost if he chooses that option. At the end of the visit, Bill's doctor electronically prescribes a pain medication and is able to save him twenty dollars by prescribing a medication on the health plan's formulary (list of approved medications). Before leaving the doctor's office, Sarah's husband agrees to pay the one hundred dollars owed for the visit. He received an estimate for this amount in advance, so he knew how much he would have to pay. Shortly after his visit, Bill receives a follow-up e-mail that includes a note from his doctor along with some additional information about back pain management. And they discuss his progress during a scheduled web visit. Bill also receives, via his cell phone, regular reminders to refill his pain medication.

Over the course of the year, Sarah's health plan works together with her and her family's providers to assess how family members are progressing toward the destinations on their healthcare itineraries or health improvement plans.

Seeking Assistance with Questions

Sarah used to dread calling her health plan with questions because the customer service staff often did not know the answers. But things are different now because the customer service department has information about Sarah's health improvement plan, her funding sources (such as her health savings account), and other relevant information and seems to welcome the opportunity to interact with Sarah. For example, when Sarah calls her health plan about a benefit question, the customer service representatives access her records and remind her to schedule her annual mammogram. Sometimes they even send a follow-up e-mail alert about opportunities for her to save money, such as by completing an annual health risk assessment on a timely basis. Sarah spends a lot of time outside her house, so she prefers text messages as a way to get reminders about filling prescriptions. Sarah's health plan tries to give her and her family information in the ways they prefer rather than in a mass mailing or generic communication to all of its members.

When Sarah looks back at her healthcare experience over the past year, she feels confident about her more active role. She is relieved that her benefits plan now covers the care that her family most needs, such as proven asthma therapy and supplies. Because her daughter's asthma is under control, Sarah misses fewer days from work. Sarah and her husband are pleased with the decisions they have made about his back pain treatment. And with the help of his health coach, doctor, and online educational tools, his back is improving, and he even received one hundred dollars in cash for achieving his weight loss goal. Sarah no longer dreads calling her health plan with questions because not only do the staff members answer her benefit, care, and financial questions, but they also direct her to online information and send her reminders and alerts that are personalized to her family's needs and health improvement goals. Above all, Sarah feels that the good healthcare decisions she and her family have made have resulted in savings and better health. (To see a video of Sarah's world, visit www.trizetto.com/ihm and select "Helping Consumers Make Healthier Decisions.")

Information Technology Powers Industry Transformation

Taking a systems approach to solving the healthcare crisis cannot be done with paper and telephones; rather, we must embrace the tools of this powerful age of information. Technology will enable change in healthcare just as it helped Japanese automakers transform their manufacturing and distribution processes. Technology can be used to break down the information silos that exist today to deliver comprehensive, useful information to constituents when and where they need it and in the most helpful way. As a result, a greater degree of transparency—complete information that is shared among constituents—will be achieved. Transparency is most obvious in pricing. If consumers and providers have the same understanding about how much of the cost of care the consumer will pay and how much the health plan will pay, the provider can collect payment from the consumer right at the time of the appointment. Another example of transparency is the health improvement plan that the doctor and the health plan will develop for each consumer, based on evidence-based medicine guidelines. For example, if a patient has type 2 diabetes, both he and his doctor will have the same understanding of the patient's dietary restrictions and how often he should check his glucose level. This transparency will allow patients and doctors to work toward the same goal and to talk about behaviors that follow evidence-based medicine guidelines (such as those for exercise, diet, and preventive drugs).

In addition to making transparency possible, technology will fuel systematic health management by distributing evidence-based medicine guidelines within patients' health improvement plans. Rather than hoping doctors and patients will find these guidelines on their own and follow them (as is the case today), IHM technology will present guidelines that patients can follow alongside their health improvement goals and treatment options so patients and doctors can discuss them together and be compensated for following them. We can think of this step as an electronic checklist of sorts, listing the steps that should be followed and then checking them off and compensating providers and consumers for following them.

With the current national focus on electronic health records, we must understand exactly what these records will and will not accomplish with regard to achieving IHM. Electronic health records are an excellent way to maintain an ongoing record of a patient's medical care over time. They can also help address certain patient safety issues, such as allergic reactions to medications. Over time, electronic health records will ensure that evidence-based medicine is practiced more consistently. However, in order for electronic records to contribute the most toward achieving IHM, they must be viewed as one part of a larger enterprise information design that includes benefit plans tailored to each consumer, aligned incentives for physicians and consumers, and, of course, the recommended care guidelines that will improve health and reduce cost.

Other types of electronic records technology such as the long-awaited personal health records (described in greater detail in chapter 9) will help complete the system, along with many other creative applications of technology, such as social media. In other words, creating good information systems that engage and assist both providers and consumers in healthcare decision making is essential to the achievement of IHM.

How IHM Will Save Money

We just saw how Sarah and her family reduced their healthcare costs while also improving their health. Would it surprise you to learn that if Integrated Healthcare Management were to be implemented across the US population, we could knock 20–30 percent off the total cost of healthcare?[2] A field study analysis using actual claims and experience data from US health plans shows that the application of even basic IHM principles would result in savings of 10 percent of total commercial medical costs.[3] If you extrapolate this number over 150 million employer-sponsored beneficiaries (at the time of the study), it would result in projected savings of $72.7 billion.[4] The study's projected savings would come from the following major categories:

- Three percent of the savings would come from consumer-focused programs targeting wellness, health improvement, and education (such as obesity management and smoking cessation).
- Thirty-three percent of the savings would come from consumer-focused programs that target informed decision making and improved treatment compliance and are reinforced through value-based benefits (such as low back pain treatment and preventive drug regimens).
- Thirty-five percent of the savings would come from decreased provider practice variation and a move to evidence-based medicine through electronic health records and value-based reimbursement.
- Twenty-nine percent of the savings would come from increased provider focus on treatment management and care coordination for patients with more complex conditions (such as people who have a combination of diabetes, congestive heart failure, and chronic obstructive pulmonary disease).

The greatest savings opportunities in IHM come from consumers who have more than one late-stage condition such as the ones just described (e.g., both diabetes and congestive heart failure).

Who Can Lead the Way to IHM?

IHM provides a framework for consumers, providers, employers, brokers, and health plans to work toward the same goals. As we saw in chapter 7, healthcare is currently a politically charged zero-sum game. Consequently, much energy is expended debating the motivation of health plans and providers or the trust (or lack thereof) that consumers have in different parts of the system. This debate is irresolvable, and it just encourages constituents and policy makers to take potshots at one another. The reality is that consumers regard information they receive from their doctor (regardless of its original source) as more reliable than if they receive the same information from other sources, so it makes sense to develop a system that fosters patient-doctor dialogue and partnership. Integrated Healthcare Management will use technology to give patients and doctors shared information based on evidence-based medicine, value-based benefits, and value-based provider reimbursements, thereby making systematic health management a reality.

In general, entities that touch the most parts of the healthcare elephant are best able to design benefits, design reimbursements, set up high-level systematic care plans, and automate evidence-based medicine into work flow. Therefore, health plans and integrated delivery systems are best positioned to take on this role. Individual providers or even providers loosely affiliated around a hospital are unlikely to be able to implement IHM, because most do not have the required level of coordination of benefits and care on behalf of the consumer. Nor do they have the baseline information capabilities that connect consumers, providers, employers, and brokers into an organized supply chain, which is required for putting IHM in motion. In addition, health plans already have data about interactions among consumers and providers as well as detailed benefit information, all of which would serve as the foundation for this new approach. As I mentioned earlier, Accountable Care Organizations (ACOs) will have to climb most or all of the supply-chain management hill in order to assemble the same type of information infrastructure that health plans already have for efficiently managing populations.

As we saw in chapter 7, through automation and other technological advances, health plans have made great strides in reducing the portion of the healthcare dollar that is spent on benefit administration. It is not difficult to imagine different ways for health plans to use their infrastructure collaboratively to help organizations achieve IHM. For example, health plans could provide the administrative capabilities for ACOs to enroll members, pay claims, answer customer inquiries, and provide disease management and health and wellness programs. Whether on their own or in collaboration with providers, health plans' facility with technology and their position at the center of the healthcare supply chain provide opportunities for them to continue to innovate ways that consumers, providers, employers, and brokers can improve care and reduce costs.

Making the Jump from the Healthcare Jungle to IHM

As you can see, Integrated Healthcare Management has the potential to transform the US healthcare system, reducing skyrocketing costs, and improving quality of care.

And just as the roles and responsibilities of the other healthcare constituents will change with the IHM approach, so, too, will the role of the health plan. While health plans are positioned well in the supply chain to drive change, they will have to make some significant changes themselves in order for IHM to succeed. Health plans will have to shift their role from that of claims processor to one of collaborative health and wellness facilitator. They will need to focus on whole-person care—becoming a patient's advocate over time and across medical conditions—rather than simply collecting premiums and paying out claims for care in the short term. Health plans will have to create a culture of health rather than focusing, as they do today, mainly on reimbursing for treating illness. In this culture of health, they will create a healthcare improvement plan for each and every patient so that not only will the sick receive the treatment recommended for their condition, but the healthy will receive support and services that evidence-based medicine has shown can help them optimize their health. Health plans will systematically remind patients and their providers to schedule preventive screenings (such as mammograms, colonoscopy tests, and Pap tests). Health plans will also use information technology to track how well a patient is progressing toward her health goals (such as weight management, exercise, blood pressure, and cholesterol), and they will systematically notify consumers about health education programs related to each consumer's specific health goals, as well as ways consumers can lower healthcare costs. Finally, in the IHM culture of health, those plans will reward consumers and doctors financially for following evidence-based recommendations that are likely to lead to better health.

While health plans will manage the distribution of information, create incentives for providers and consumers to follow a shared healthcare itinerary based on evidence-based guidelines, continuously monitor how well consumers are doing in meeting their healthcare goals, and provide support to consumers and other constituents, they will not in any way be regarded as a substitute for highly trained physicians. Nor will health plan information technology (including the personal health record) be a substitute for electronic health records within doctors' offices and hospitals. These information technology solutions will reinforce one another. In the IHM world, health plans will drive the healthcare system and help each element of the system interact more smoothly and effectively; however, physicians will maintain their sacred role in providing care to patients. My hope is that by using the IHM approach, the historically adversarial relationship between health plans and providers will give way to a cooperative era in which the information that health plans add to the equation will empower physicians as the quarterbacks of systematic healthcare management.

EHRs, PHRs, EMRs—what are these confusing acronyms? And why are they such a central part of the current healthcare debate? In chapter 9, we will take a look at these repositories of patient health information, how they can reduce waste and decrease the number of medical errors, and how PHRs can be implemented more quickly than other types of electronic records.

Chapter 9

Digital Alphabet Soup:
Understanding EHRs, EMRs, and PHRs

What's in a name? That which we call a rose
By any other name would smell as sweet.

—William Shakespeare, *Romeo and Juliet*

R aise the subject of improving the US healthcare system, and you
will undoubtedly spark a discussion about healthcare information
technology, regardless of your political leanings or where you live. In the
popular press, healthcare information technology has become synonymous
with the concept of electronic health records (EHRs). Moreover, many
people believe that if health records can be computerized (digitized) and
shared (according to appropriate security and confidentiality rules), they
will help solve both cost and quality problems in healthcare. It is interesting
to note that because the federal government has allotted large sums of
money to promote the adoption of EHRs, nearly every major technology
company and every other company remotely associated with healthcare
suddenly has an EHR solution they believe is worthy of consideration and
reimbursement. I'm reminded of the flurry of activity surrounding the initial commercial development of the Internet in the late 1990s, and how
even though enormous capital was applied to make the Internet communications channel into a useful and powerful tool, only a small handful of
companies developed solutions that survive today.

The fact is, while electronic records will be a key component in
improving the US healthcare system, it is only part of the solution—and
not as big a part as many people might think. Implementing a meaningful,

sustainable solution requires a combination of people (that is, the constituents we discussed in chapter 5), processes, *and* technology. And having read the book to this point, you likely understand that if you try to solve a specific problem only by implementing technology, even if that technology is very advanced, it is simply an applied technology (e.g., the use of EHRs to reduce the chance of medication errors).

In order to change the US healthcare system in a coordinated, systematic way, we must incorporate applied technologies as pieces of an overall enterprise information systems design that considers all requirements of the system, including different incentives that encourage behaviors on the part of all constituents and that will give consumers the best healthcare value for every dollar spent. Improving healthcare through Integrated Healthcare Management is a perfect example because it goes beyond simply computerizing existing paper records (paving cow paths). Instead, the Integrated Healthcare Management approach also incorporates incentives for both doctors and consumers to move consumers toward their individual health improvement goals. The information technology used in IHM includes not only electronic health records that store information about patients' conditions, medications, and treatment in the past, but also a health improvement plan (health itinerary) that provides information helpful in weighing treatment options, reminds patients to fill prescriptions or make appointments, and alerts doctors when patients have missed a step on their health improvement plans. IHM healthcare information systems incorporate some of the enterprise concepts we see in supermarkets or big-box stores, in which information is used to actively engage consumers, and it also takes a page from virtual stores that acknowledge that information from different sources may have to be pulled together for the consumer.

In chapter 8, I outlined important principles of an overall information technology systems design that must be included if we are to improve healthcare in the United States in a systematic and sustainable way. To refresh your memory before we discuss the various types of electronic health records, here are the main principles of IHM:

- *Value-based benefits* are benefits designed to encourage consumers to make choices that scientifically have been shown to lead to healthier outcomes.
- *Value-based reimbursement* is paying doctors for results (for following evidence-based medicine guidelines) rather than for how much treatment they provide.
- *Systematic health management* means looking across populations of people—from the healthy to the chronically ill—to help healthy people stay healthy, sick people not get sicker, and patients along the entire spectrum improve their health status. Systematic health management includes developing a health improvement plan or patient itinerary for each patient.
- *Evidence-based medicine guidelines* are treatments that have been shown by peer-reviewed scientific research to be comparatively more effective than other methods.
- *Culture of health* is an environment where everyone—consumers, providers, employers, and brokers—consciously works to improve health status and control costs, both individually and collectively.

Certainly, developing a system using these principles is a tall order, and even with the significant existing information capabilities of private payers and integrated delivery systems, our nation will not get there overnight. Therefore, sensible steps that create the energy and will to move our healthcare system in this direction, such as the attention being given to electronic health records by President Barack Obama (and President George W. Bush before him), will help fuel progress. However, for the typical consumer, not to mention health professionals and policy makers, it is important to understand what we are seeking if we are to meet or exceed expectations regarding the promise of electronic health records. President John F. Kennedy's goal of reaching the moon was systematically far less complicated than today's call to provide accessible, affordable, and high-quality healthcare for all Americans.

This chapter will discuss both the promise and the misconceptions of the use of EHRs and will make a strong case for how one "cousin" of the

EHR, known as the personal health record (PHR), can be applied immediately and relatively inexpensively to move us toward Integrated Healthcare Management while complementing initiatives under way in hospitals and physician offices.

First, let's clarify the alphabet soup of EHRs, EMRs, and PHRs being discussed with regard to health records. These acronyms refer to just three of the many different types of health records either in use today or being developed, and many people are confused as to which is which. *Electronic health record (EHR)* is the term you see in the news most often, as it has become the subject of government healthcare reform and has therefore entered the public lexicon. *Electronic medical records (EMRs)*, which are used primarily in hospital settings, are hospital visit–specific, and are in fairly widespread use today, particularly in integrated delivery systems. *Personal health records (PHRs)* typically are designed to be used by both consumers and providers. Like EHRs and EMRs, PHRs are being implemented and adopted at various rates across the country. Yet by their very nature, PHRs offer an opportunity to accelerate the progress toward Integrated Healthcare Management.

A Closer Look at EMRs, EHRs, and PHRs

EMRs: Electronic Records—Usually Hospital/Clinic-Centered

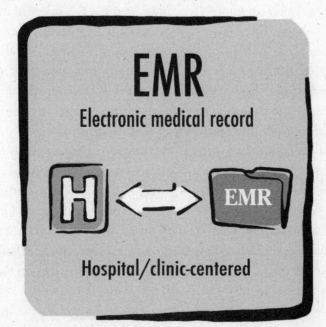

In the hospital and advanced clinical setting, which can be very complex, the electronic record system (the EMR) needs to provide all the vital data about patients, no matter where they go within the hospital—from the operating room to the MRI machine to the hospital room. The hospital record contains clinical data geared to the expertise level of the treating physicians and nurses throughout the hospital, including numerous specialists. The EMR typically is designed to highlight data for one relatively contained episode of care in one particular hospital organization. In some cases, the record also includes (or enables treating physicians to access) historical data from treatment centers and practices that are affiliated with the hospital in which the patient is being treated.

The EMR is a deep record in that it contains a tremendous amount of detail, potentially including data-intensive lab results; patient readings; and X-rays, MRI tests, or other diagnostic images used in determining or adjusting treatment at any point in time or location within the hospital. The format of the EMR is designed to be understood by healthcare professionals, not typical consumers like you and me, nor is it intended to be distributed outside that narrow clinical setting. Improving patient safety during a hospital visit is a vitally important goal of hospital-based electronic medical records. Many hospital care processes (or work flows) differ widely from those in other healthcare settings, and even those in other hospitals. Therefore, patient data must be updated very quickly because hospitalized patients are often in life-threatening or acute situations.

As we saw in chapter 6, even within a single hospital there may be many different EMRs within different departments, each storing data in a separate information silo. For example, it is not uncommon to find separate records systems in radiology, pathology, and other key hospital functions. Often, doctors and other hospital staff must log onto each of these systems separately and connect the dots themselves when making healthcare decisions. And we will recall from chapter 4 that many physicians in most hospitals also are part of private practices, which may use other types of health records. While today's EMR is far from an ideal systematic and integrated record system, it is vitally important in enabling complex care settings such as hospitals to function safely and efficiently. Over time, as more hospitals come online with this important tool, the detailed clinical data must be integrated with other healthcare information systems at physicians' offices and health plans to better support patients receiving care in hospitals. Adding to the systematic complexity of EMRs, once-monolithic general hospitals throughout the country are remaking themselves into a combination of centers of excellence and coordinated care entities such as Accountable Care Organizations (ACOs), so the work processes in these organizations are changing from those of traditional hospitals. As a result, just as some hospitals are getting their arms around a common EMR system to break down their own internal information silos, in their new role as ACOs, they will have to become more like health plans as they manage the entire supply chain and think about providing a full spectrum of care to patients. Naturally, their information systems also will have to support the additional work processes involved in being an ACO.

EHRs: Electronic Records in Physician Offices

Information needs and care processes in the doctor's office are often very different from those in the hospital, and they also vary greatly among different types of physician practices. As we've discussed, physicians practice in a variety of setting types, ranging from one- and two-person practices to very large integrated delivery systems with outpatient facilities such as Kaiser or the Veterans Administration (VA). Because of the diversity of size, complexity, and resource support, the information capabilities available to physicians naturally vary. For example, a rural doctor likely has no dedicated information technology staff, while an integrated delivery system likely has an entire dedicated department. Electronic health records for a physician practice can be as simple as turning paper charts into electronic documents for easy retrieval. More advanced record systems integrate multiple physician office functions, such as medical records, order entry, results reporting, appointment scheduling, and insurance and patient billing. These advanced, integrated EHR systems are especially useful for multispecialty group practices in which primary care physicians and specialists coordinate care among themselves as well as with their on-site lab and pharmacy. A recent survey conducted by the Centers for Disease Control and Prevention's National Center for Health Statistics found that just under 25 percent of physicians have adopted a basic type of EHR, and approximately 10 percent say they have adopted the more advanced, integrated form.[1] Although this represents progress, the reality is that it will take tremendous time and effort to create electronic records for every physician practice.

In contrast to the hospital-based record, the practice-based electronic health record is designed to give the doctor a longer-term view of the patient, usually the length of the relationship between the patient and physician. Patients receiving treatment in the office setting typically have less-critical conditions than those receiving treatment in the hospital. For example, they may go to their doctor's office for routine examinations or for ongoing treatment for chronic conditions. These scenarios require care management over a much longer period of time than for an acute care hospital situation, so most EHRs keep track of a patient's medical care with a particular practice over the entire time the patient goes to that practice. In addition, record systems in physician practices are designed to be used by a more limited number of staff, who tend to be familiar with one another, and many of whom deal with less day-to-day clinical intensity than their hospital counterparts.

Some healthcare advocates have suggested that physician-based EHRs should be transportable and shareable across the healthcare supply chain to eliminate errors and redundancy. Systematically, one needs to consider whether using records in that manner is in line with physicians' objectives for their own record systems and work flow. It should be pretty easy to understand that the work flow in an orthopedic specialist's office is (and should remain) very different from that of an oncologist or a primary care physician and that the orthopedist may need a different set of information than the primary care doctor. Given the variation in the information each type of doctor may need, the best compromise is to create standardized data formats within differing EHR systems so that each type of record solution can draw in the data and present them in a format that is familiar to the clinician viewing the record. There is a significant amount of work to be done to develop EHRs based in physician offices so that they ultimately improve quality and help the office run more smoothly without simply increasing overhead.

PHRs: Electronic Records across Physician Offices, Hospitals, and Other Caregivers

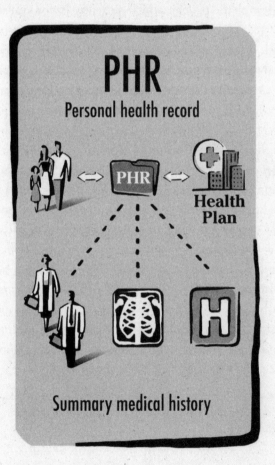

The third type of electronic health record is the personal health record (PHR). There are many variations of this type of record, ranging from the do-it-yourself variety, where consumers enter data about their health history and care, to record systems in which the key data are automatically fed from other sources in the healthcare system (for example, by a health plan). Because PHRs are Internet-based, they can be viewed from any location and, in compliance with security and privacy protections, can be seen by anyone who is authorized to see them.

The simplest way to think about a PHR is as an outline of your healthcare history—your health résumé. Certain types of PHRs provide a comprehensive view of the patient, which currently is not available from any other type of record. Unlike today's hospital- and physician-based medical records, which contain information only from affiliated locations (at best), the PHR can provide a comprehensive overview of all diagnoses, procedures, testing, and treatments that covers all locations and providers. The PHR does not necessarily contain test results or detailed notes on treatment (although it can); rather, it lists the types of tests performed, their dates, and the names of the providers by whom they were ordered and performed. This summary-level information can act as a prompt for doctors to get more detailed information if they need it. The PHR's breadth helps physicians and others throughout the healthcare supply chain identify potential drug interactions, avoid duplicate testing, make comparative evaluations, and cross-check the care you are receiving across all your treatment centers.

Another important advantage of the PHR is that it can be understood easily by consumers and providers alike. All of the physicians, nurses, and therapists involved in your care (and even your own family members, with your permission) are capable of using it. Because it is in summary form, the PHR is useful in a wide variety of settings, including your home, the doctor's office, and when you first arrive at a hospital for treatment.

One Size Does Not Fit All

In chapter 4 we saw that big-box supply-chain organizers such as Walmart utilize enterprise information to create high efficiency within their four walls. We learned that Amazon uses information technology to create a virtual supply chain for consumers that is not dependent upon physical location. Just as retailers use different models for organizing and managing supply chains, the US healthcare system's varied and expanding range of delivery models will likely require differing electronic health record solutions to handle the full range of healthcare benefits and delivery methods across the system. In other words, a one-size-fits-all approach to clinical electronic health records will not deliver the system-wide cost, quality, and access improvements we seek.

Having been behind the firewalls and in the shoes of many different healthcare constituents, I can personally attest to the need for multiple health record models that are integrated with one another. I was involved in the implementation of the earliest electronic medical records and physician records in integrated delivery networks; I've been a patient on the receiving end (both good and bad) of the information in these records; I have accompanied primary and specialty physicians going about their daily work; and as a board member of a hospital, I maintain familiarity with current health record implementation initiatives. Given the wide spectrum of information needs across healthcare constituents and the differences in how their work flows and computer systems are designed, it is clear that we will need to employ multiple types of records, but we must also make sure they are linked and coordinated appropriately within the construct of Integrated Healthcare Management. We cannot lose sight of the ultimate objective of health record systems: better coordination of benefits and care at the right time and place in the consumer (patient) and provider interaction.

The Dream: National and Regional Health Information Exchanges

If you step back from the complexity I just described, it is probably easy to see why many people who do not have a detailed understanding of the entire healthcare supply chain are euphoric about the possibilities represented by regional and national health information exchanges (HIEs). When people think about HIEs, they most commonly envision a system where EHR and EMR data from any source can be brought together whenever and wherever they are needed. Having different EMR and EHR systems work together seamlessly, regardless of what software vendor may have created the electronic records system, is commonly referred to as *interoperability*. So, HIEs are generally thought of as a collection of interoperable (compatible) EHRs and EMRs. The classic story used to make this case is about a person who has an accident while on vacation in another state and is "saved" because his medication history is instantaneously available to the emergency room physician who is viewing the patient's health record online as the patient arrives. Another version explains how the chest image of a vacationing tourist is retrieved from her doctor's office across the country, allowing the patient to be diagnosed and treated rapidly and thus avoiding a potentially fatal aneurysm. A less dramatic example would be if a local community hospital were able to share lab results from inside the hospital with the cardiologist who referred the patient to the hospital so he could track his patient's progress following a heart attack. To be clear, I am in favor of such capabilities, and as a patient myself, I hope for the day when these types of stories become routine. However, much more is involved than most people think. Specifically, the base data (some handwritten) in every doctor's office and hospital would need to be digitized (entered into a computer system); the way data are stored and formatted would need to be standardized across all EHR and EMR solutions and locations; the HIE would need to be able to precisely identify the requestor and source of the data to ensure that the information reaches the right place; and security measures would have to be designed to ensure that the requestor was authorized to see the data in order to ensure privacy. While the concept of multiple record systems that can share information makes good sense, creating this information utopia is not as easy as it may seem. The political controversy over who administers the connected sharing of such data is why so many local, regional, and national models and efforts have emerged. In fact, interoperability has never existed across nonaffiliated entities in any industry to the degree people are calling for in healthcare.

Looking at a few examples in industries that have fairly advanced information technology systems may help to make my point. Many people like to use banking as an example of an industry with this type of interoperability. Their rationale is that you can retrieve cash from any ATM in the world as long as you have money or credit. But this example is not truly analogous to the interoperable electronic health record examples I just described. Sending information to facilitate the transfer of cash balances among different institutions' accounts is a relatively simple transaction, like sending an electronic prescription to a pharmacy or checking insurance eligibility—healthcare transactions already in daily use.

One analogy I can think of to suggest the level of healthcare record interoperability some seek is the following hypothetical example. Suppose you had a brokerage account at Merrill Lynch with fixed-income bonds that are actively traded and therefore constantly changing, a brokerage account at Morgan Stanley Smith Barney with a portfolio of stocks that are actively traded, a checking account at Bank of America, two savings accounts at your local credit union, and an options and commodities trading account with Citigroup. Now, suppose you want to instantly be able to look across the detailed history and current activity of all the investments and accounts from one system and make that information available (with proper security, of course) to any professional in any of those financial institutions. The fact is that such a capability does not exist. Each bank has proprietary ways of formatting and displaying data to consumers and also for internal purposes, which is why the banking industry has not reached the level of complete interoperability in the hypothetical situation described. And even though Walmart or Toyota can efficiently exchange electronic information with its suppliers, Walmart is not likely to try to interoperate your purchase data with Amazon or Target.

The Federal Aviation Administration (FAA) air traffic control system is another example held up as supposedly interoperable, but it is actually a command and control system and could only work under a central controlling authority—that is, the government. The FAA system has the appearance of interoperability because every airline *seems* connected despite their being completely different companies. However, in reality this system relies upon a mandated regulatory transmission of electronic signals by all aircrafts, a centrally controlled radar system, and highly trained pilots who must obey instructions from other humans (e.g., air traffic controllers).

Information technologists (because they truly believe it) will almost always tell those who seek to share information across disparate systems that a layer of software can be built to make things interoperable, as long as common data standards exist. This claim may be true for static data—data that don't change very often and that need to be pulled together from disparate sources, such as matching a doctor's name on an insurance claim with that doctor's name on a health record. But once data "go in motion"—meaning they get changed along different steps in a process—and another part of the process is not aware of the change, then things can easily go awry. For example, one doctor prescribes a particular drug on Monday, but the patient does not fill the prescription right away (meaning the pharmacy has not yet submitted a claim that denotes the prescription has been filled), and then the patient sees another doctor on Wednesday, who does not have the information about what the first doctor prescribed. Without too much imagination, you can see how both the benefits data and the care management data can get out of whack and cause both consumers and their doctors to get confused.

Does this mean we should give up on connected EHRs that can be shared among providers and consumers? Absolutely not. But we do have to take a step back from the problem to be able to solve it. From a systematic viewpoint, the first relevant question is around which constituent to center the health record. This answer is obvious—it's the consumer. The next relevant question is which constituent has data containing the fullest view of the consumer. As we will see, except in the case of a single-payer situation (like the VA) or an integrated delivery system that also runs its own health plan (such as Kaiser), the systematic answer to the question is private payers (health plans). As we will recall from chapter 6, private payers have an abundance of fully digitized benefits data that reflect the diagnoses and care received across all care settings.

Acknowledging the Data Accuracy Debate

Let me restate, for clarity, that I am not suggesting that the payer-based PHR is a substitute or clinical equivalent to hospital-based records and records based in a physician office, but it is a powerful jump start for achieving the goal of patient-centered connected records. In my twenty-plus years of implementing clinical and administrative information systems, I have heard the same arguments from physicians time and time again about poor data quality—that some of the data (and therefore the information produced by the data) are just plain wrong. These physicians are absolutely right! Ironically, these same physicians are often the origin of the wrong data, and they know precisely what coding limitations or less-than-perfect entry processes cause the data to be in error. For example, some physicians may want to document health information that is more specific than what is available within the coding options today, such as whether the underlying cause of an injury to a limb is work related, due to an auto accident, or related to sports or recreation. In addition, in order to maximize their reimbursement, sometimes doctors enter codes that indicate a slightly higher level of severity or time spent with the patient than what actually occurred, or they may break out a discrete bundled code such as an appendectomy into many smaller coding units. The good news is that most everyone agrees that more specificity and accuracy in codes is desirable, and the federal government has called for providers to submit claims using an updated set of codes that include these nuances. Even with some of these challenges to the accuracy of payer data derived from claims submitted by providers, the overarching point is that electronic payer data are mostly correct, point in the right direction, and can add great value to the overall system, as long as they are kept in context and applied judiciously in the work flow.

PHRs: Getting There Faster, Cheaper, and Better

As of now, nearly all types of electronic health record systems are still in the early stages of being implemented, even though there are notable industry leaders who serve mostly larger provider and payer organizations and have implemented excellent record solutions. To accelerate the rate at which electronic records are adopted, the American Recovery and Reinvestment Act, passed in Congress in February 2009, provides payment incentives for providers who incorporate EHRs into their practices. Today, approximately

25 percent of physician practices have adopted a basic form of EHR.[2] The goal of this legislation is to increase that figure to nearly 100 percent within five years. In reality, I believe achieving this important goal in clinical settings is likely to take more than a decade. But that does not mean we should delay implementation, nor does it mean we must wait ten years or more to achieve the objective of delivering better information accurately and consistently to every patient/caregiver interaction.

To understand how we can accomplish the goal of implementing PHRs, let's review some of the concepts from this book. First, take another look at the supply-chain picture below, and keep in mind that private payers administer benefits for more than two hundred million Americans.

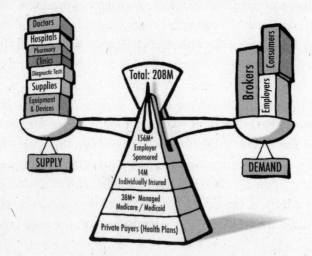

Now let's take another look at how the healthcare premium dollar[3] is distributed (from chapter 7). From a systematic standpoint, it should be clear that the healthcare dollar flows through the payer and is distributed to the "supply side" of the supply chain. In order to get reimbursed their portion of the dollar, the physicians, hospitals, diagnostic testing centers, pharmacies, and retail clinics submit claims to the payer, who then has a record of all of this activity at the individual consumer level. These data are close to 100 percent digitized, since the industry has been encouraging the use of electronic payment data for many years.

The Healthcare Dollar
from a Payer Perspective

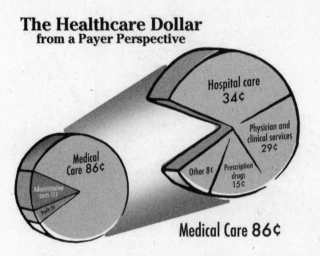

Hospital care
34¢

Physician and
clinical services
29¢

Medical
Care 86¢

Administrative
costs 11¢

Profit 3¢

Other 8¢

Prescription
drugs
15¢

Medical Care 86¢

Now let's take another look at the information silos discussed in chapter 6.

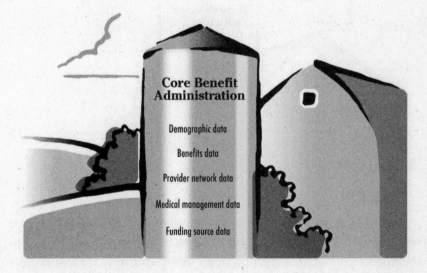

**Core Benefit
Administration**

Demographic data

Benefits data

Provider network data

Medical management data

Funding source data

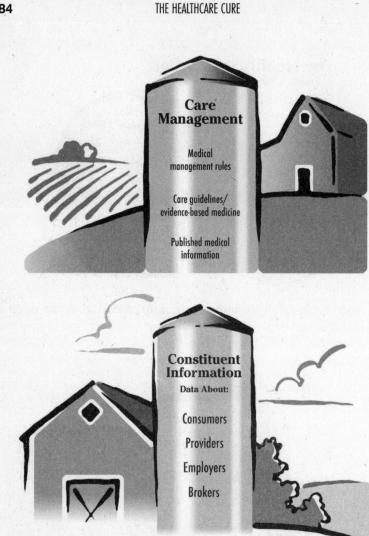

As you can see, the data contained in just the core benefits administration silo are a rich source of information that can be used in a health record to show the health history (diagnoses and treatments) for a particular patient. The payers also have data in the other information silos that can be used to enrich electronic health records (more about that in a moment). Let's add one more illustration to show the relationship between the payer-based PHR and other data sources. Your answers to several straightforward questions will help explain this illustration.

1. In a given year, do you typically see multiple doctors in different practices?
2. In a typical year, do you receive care at multiple medical facilities (offices)?
3. Do you have diagnostic tests (e.g., blood work or imaging) at still other locations?
4. Do you get your prescriptions filled at one or more retail pharmacy locations?

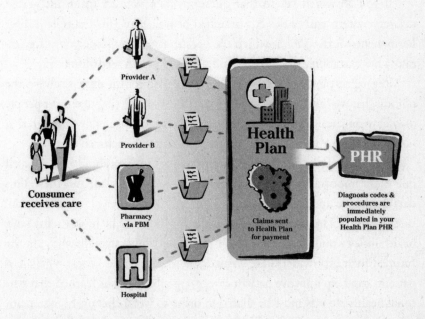

If you are a typical US healthcare consumer, you answered yes to all four questions. If you answered yes to *any* of the first four questions (which puts you in the company of the majority of Americans), then your health plan is likely in the best position to create your PHR because it collects digitized data from multiple doctors, hospitals, diagnostic testing centers, and pharmacies so it can be shared among you, your physician(s), and other caregivers.

If, on the other hand, you were able to answer no to *all* four questions, then you probably receive your care in an integrated delivery system (such as the Mayo Clinic) that coordinates the supply side of the supply chain on your behalf and can probably produce a relatively complete personal health record for you.

Now let's ask a fifth question:

5. Are your health insurance benefits administered by the same organization that is providing you the care outlined above?

If you answered yes to that question, then you are in an integrated delivery system with a directly attached benefit plan (for example, Kaiser Permanente or the VA) in which the organization providing your care certainly has the ability to create a good personal health record for you.

Regardless of which category you ended up in for the exercise above, the point is that we can and should all have PHRs. Considering that most people only have one health plan in a given year, and so much data flow through that health plan, the absence of a PHR is a waste of good, digitized data.

If you have followed the logic to this point, then you should ask yourself one more important question: If I change my health plan, and the claims data that make up my health history don't follow me to my new health plan, isn't that bad? The answer is yes. In order for PHRs to be most useful, your health history must be transportable to any health plan you may join in the future. Much as providers have learned that sharing clinical data on behalf of patients can help improve patient care, so, too, have payers learned that personal health records must be shared in order to work effectively. Systematically, the transportability of PHRs is quicker and more practical than interoperability. This is because payers are accustomed to having consumers added to and deleted from their membership rolls each year and could also transfer patient records when patients switch health plans.

Remember, IHM Is Benefits *and* Care

The description above illustrates how all the data from nearly every significant point at which we as consumers touch the healthcare system are funneled through the health insurance payment system. This process has been in effect for decades because care providers throughout the healthcare delivery system submit patient encounter and claims data in order to get paid. As a result, our healthcare system already has tremendous digitized health history that, if put into the form of a personal health record, could start delivering better information to patients and doctors during every visit or interaction.

However, clinical data alone from these record systems, while helpful, are not enough. To give patients and doctors a full picture of the patient health status, clinical data must be integrated with benefits information. For example, it's not all that useful to the patient if the doctor recommends a treatment that isn't covered by the patient's insurance and that he cannot afford on his own. Nor would the patient be well served if his doctor were to refer him to a specialist who is not part of his health plan's approved network.

In addition to being able to integrate benefits information with clinical data, a well-designed PHR should enable providers to know which communication methods each patient prefers for receiving information about healthcare. For example, a web-based personal health record with physician-guided content and e-mail reminders can be a great tool, except when your patient is an eighty-five-year-old senior who doesn't often use a computer. And when collecting information about these communications preferences, PHRs should not assume that all consumers have reliable access to computers. While many of us are able to enter that information on the PHR's website, information about how we as consumers prefer to receive information from providers can just as easily be obtained at benefits enrollment time, whether that's online, on paper, or by phone.

It is also important that data contained in PHRs be comprehensive, relevant, and current. Today, providers and pharmacists are naturally motivated to enter and transmit as quickly as possible the data that lead to payment for their services. Even claims that are submitted on paper are systematically digitized by health insurers, meaning that nearly 100 percent of health insurance claims data are available for PHRs. As I mentioned earlier, payer-based PHRs are no substitute for hospital-based and physician-office-based record systems. In both of these cases, the healthcare activities and results may be flowing just minutes apart. A PHR is not intended to keep up with the pace of the physician's or office's work flow, but when the visit or procedure is completed, the data from that care should feed the PHR and update the consumer's health résumé.

To be fully effective as a tool for caregivers and patients, summary health background information must be available anytime and anywhere. Most PHRs include the Internet as one option for viewing health records: so as long as the consumer, physician, or other caregiver has an Internet connection and the proper security, he can access the record. EHRs and EMRs, on the other hand, use information that is specific to the day-to-day (even minute-to-minute) work flows in doctors' offices and hospitals; because that information is highly detailed and constantly changing during the course of an office visit or procedure, the EHR and EMR systems cannot easily provide a broad view of the patient across multiple and nonaffiliated locations over the Internet the way the PHR can.

Let's Not Forget Security and Privacy

Most EHR, EMR, and PHR systems have strong data security safeguards, such as encryption, to prevent random hacking or unintended distribution (such as when a personal computer and its hard drive are stolen). However, the treatment of information privacy and control for authorized users is not so clear cut. This topic is important for all of us as healthcare consumers. Right now, there is a debate among both advocates and developers of all types of electronic health records about privacy and who should have control over the data. Some people are advocating that under current privacy laws, electronic health records could be shared among doctors and other treatment centers without specific permission from, or even knowledge by, the patient. Others advocate that consumers should always be in control of the distribution of all or parts of their health information, except in extreme circumstances, such as when a patient is unconscious in the emergency room. Rather than this debate turning into a battle that pits healthcare providers against consumer and privacy advocacy groups, it should be reframed in the context of supporting and understanding current Health Insurance Portability and Accountability Act (HIPAA) regulations. These regulations allow for the authorized flow of healthcare information among HIPAA entities for purposes of treating a patient, and they give patients control over the sharing of information with other entities. According to the regulations, HIPAA entities include doctors, hospitals, health plans, pharmacies, and other entities that have access to a patient's personal health information. It is important that these data do not fall into the wrong hands and that patient privacy is protected.

To a large extent, the privacy issues come down to doctor-centered versus patient-centered control. In short, it probably makes practical sense for electronic health records and electronic medical records to be more of a provider-controlled system, and for payer-based personal health records to be more of a consumer-controlled system, but both should be assumed shareable among HIPAA entities unless permission to do so is specifically turned off by the consumer. And certainly, there is a shared understanding in the medical and payer communities that in certain situations it might make sense to require an additional level of authorization from the consumer before revealing certain behavioral health information and other particularly sensitive diagnoses such as schizophrenia or AIDS. Personal health records can be designed to accommodate these levels of authorization. In fact, my company, TriZetto, has patented a process that allows consumers to grant access to different levels of their personal health information selectively via personal software keys. In my trips to Washington, DC, and in my company's participation on standards committees, I find that policy makers are doing a good job of exploring the debate over consumer and provider control of healthcare data. The issue will continue to be addressed as the specifics of healthcare reform legislation continue to be defined.

There are two final points to understand about PHRs. First, on a relative time-and-expense basis, PHRs could be in place and adopted much sooner and for a fraction of the cost of EMRs and EHRs, at least for the more than two hundred million people whose benefits are managed by private payers (and for fee-for-service Medicare beneficiaries as well). Second, the aggressive pursuit of PHRs will actually accelerate the usefulness of hospital-based EMRs and EHRs based in doctors' offices. This is because the claims data in the PHR includes the date of service, the place of service, and the treating physician, as well as the diagnoses and treatments. Thus, it can point providers to which EHRs and EMRs contain more detailed data about a particular diagnosis or treatment. In other words, the personal health record essentially creates the search parameters to track down and connect otherwise disparate data sources, similar to how keywords function in a Google® search.

Experiencing Your Personal Health Record in an IHM World

We'll conclude this chapter by describing an example of how the use of a payer-based PHR can optimize benefits and care for both the patient and the doctor.

Suppose you call a new doctor's office to make an appointment. When you arrive, instead of having to fill out all the forms about who you are, what health conditions you have, what medications you take, and who your insurance carrier and emergency contact are, the office already has that information. By the time you arrive at your doctor's office, the staff has sent a standard eligibility verification request to your health plan, which confirms that you have insurance coverage for this visit. Along with the eligibility verification that is sent back to the doctor's office comes a neatly formatted copy of your health résumé, which includes not only the information from the form but a basic summary of your health history as well.

As a result, when the nurse is checking your blood pressure and temperature, he looks at your health résumé and reads you the names and doses of prescriptions you recently filled so that all you have to do is verify that this information is accurate, rather than having to remember the names and doses of all your prescriptions. Because the nurse has accurate information about you, he is probably better able to do the initial interview with you about the reason for your visit. As the doctor walks into your examination room, she is already leafing through the personal health record that was printed when your eligibility was confirmed (or looking at it as an electronic document) and seeing what diagnoses and treatments other doctors, past and present, have made, as well as medications you have been prescribed. She notices that while you came to see her about your right knee, there was an MRI of that knee taken last year at the ski resort where you originally injured it. She seems pleased because the MRI will give you both something to compare any new diagnostic images against, and she asks her nurse to check whether he can access that image in the PHR electronically. It turns out that the clinic that performed the knee MRI has an electronic medical record and can e-mail the image in a matter of minutes.

After seeing that no severe knee injury was present on the prior image, and after physically examining you, the doctor suggests an exercise and physical therapy regimen along with a prescription to reduce the pain and inflammation around your knee. She comments that without that image, she would have sent you for a CT scan or perhaps an arthroscopic procedure by an orthopedic surgeon. You comment that the time and expense of either would have been difficult for you. Later, at the instruction of the doctor, you make an appointment with the physical therapist, who the doctor's staff has already verified is within your approved network of providers. The staff also "clicked" the contact information for the physical therapist into your PHR. At the time you make the appointment with the physical therapist, the front desk tells you exactly how much you will owe for this service. Behind the scenes, your insurance company already informed the imaging center of your financial responsibility when the physical therapist's office checked your eligibility, based on a calculation that included your covered benefits (in this case, the number of physical therapy visits you are allowed) and your deductible status (how much you have paid toward your deductible).

As part of your recovery and rehabilitation, the doctor requests that you log in to your personal health record and write down your daily rehabilitation and exercise activities for future review. These physical therapy exercises are based upon evidence-based medicine guidelines for treating the type of knee injury you have. At your follow-up visit, your physician can see on your health record how well you have done, as can other doctors you visit subsequently. In other words, the PHR can help the doctor see (and you track) how well you are complying with the recommended course of treatment. The PHR provides information that helps you choose the treatment option shown to be most effective and for which your health plan will pay (value-based benefits). The PHR also provides information to your doctor about evidence-based medicine guidelines for your injury so she can be paid for providing care that is most likely to give you the best outcome (value-based reimbursement).

Now imagine that the systems that made all this happen so smoothly were available today at no additional cost to consumers or providers. That vision is not as distant a reality as you may think. It is already being piloted by a few national health plans in selected regional markets through personal health records powered by health plan information. Is it the *perfect* answer? No. But it's a powerful start, and that's what is most important.

Moving Ahead Now

The time for the PHR is now. It presents a tremendous opportunity to improve healthcare dramatically in the near term, while the physician practice–based EHR and hospital-based EMR data become more widely implemented. Advancing personal health records now in no way impedes those other record systems; rather, it helps all three models grow together toward a fully integrated healthcare management system in the United States. The imperative heard often in Washington from everyone all the way up to President Obama seems to best summarize the case: "When it comes to addressing our healthcare challenge, we can no longer let the perfect be the enemy of the essential."[4]

Now that you have seen Sarah's world in chapter 8 and we have seen the promise of electronic health records in enhancing the dialogue and flow of information among constituents, I hope you see that our healthcare system can and will be transformed. Chapter 10 examines your changing responsibilities as a consumer of healthcare and how society can educate you in preparation for your new role.

Chapter 10

Personal Responsibility and Societal Opportunity

An individual without information cannot take responsibility; an individual who is given information cannot help but take responsibility.

—Jan Carlzon, former president and CEO of
Scandinavian Airlines System, *Moments of Truth*, 1987

Now that you have accompanied me through the healthcare jungle, you have a basic familiarity with its elements, how it works, its deficiencies and areas of strength, and how the system can be designed to provide higher-quality care at a lower cost using the Integrated Healthcare Management approach. So what does all this mean for you? Should you think differently about your role as a consumer of healthcare? By now, you may be pondering whether healthcare is an inalienable right or a staggering responsibility.

Until recently, most working and retired Americans viewed healthcare coverage as a given—something we received through our employers simply by virtue of being employed, or from the government as a present on our sixty-fifth birthday. And it was not just that coverage was readily available. For many consumers, healthcare insurance premiums also were largely paid for by employers, and the lion's share of healthcare costs were paid by health plans or, in the case of Medicare or Medicaid, the federal government. As a result, the majority of us have spent most of our lives without having to think about the actual cost of healthcare in the context of how much value it provides.

We are so sheltered from the actual costs of healthcare that most of us would fail miserably if we were to play *The Price Is Right* and asked to price healthcare procedures or prescription drugs. For example, when you are paying your $25 co-payment for your asthma inhaler, are you thinking about its "real" cost of roughly $200 for a month's supply?[1] Or if you forget to fill the asthma inhaler prescription you usually take as a preventive measure and end up in the emergency room, are you aware that the hospital will likely bill your health plan no less than $1,000 for that visit (or any emergency room visit)?[2] My own experience increased my awareness of how much prescription drugs can really cost. While on a business trip, I forgot a medication I take regularly to keep my Crohn's disease in remission and had to buy a four-day supply to last me until I got home. Who would have guessed that on a retail basis, each pill costs about $6.00? The actual cost of a one-month supply of that medication is $180, although I pay only a $10 co-payment. In addition to our lack of knowledge about how much healthcare actually costs, we are equally unaware of how widely costs can vary among different providers. In fact, an article in the *Wall Street Journal* notes that in the greater San Francisco Bay area, the cost of a colonoscopy can range from more than $700 to more than $7,000, which equals roughly a tenfold variation between the least expensive and most expensive providers.[3] Having information about the full cost of healthcare will enable us all to make more responsible decisions that will lead to better care and lower costs overall.

Awareness Increases as Healthcare Costs Rise

As insurance premiums have increased at a rate much faster than general inflation, the typical employer offering healthcare benefits has shifted a portion of this increase to employees. Consequently, consumers at all income levels have noticed that the amount they pay for healthcare is rising substantially. For some consumers, increases in their portion of the healthcare insurance premium have negated any wage increases they may have achieved (or their employers have had to hold down wage increases in order to pay rising premiums). Add to this the fact that the previously insignificant office visit and pharmacy co-payments of the 1990s have also substantially increased in most places, and deductibles have also gone up at a much faster rate than either inflation or average wage increases. If you have standard Medicare coverage (as opposed to Medicare Advantage), you now find you are financially responsible for costs beyond a certain range, particularly in buying prescription drugs. If you are in a subsidized program such as Medicaid, having access to healthcare has always been a fundamental aspect of your economic survival. With healthcare costs rising, its importance to you is now even greater. Suffice it to say that regardless of your economic status, your awareness of healthcare costs has increased. Although the same is true for employers, providers, brokers, and health plans, this chapter concentrates on how you as a consumer might contemplate your new role as a fiscally responsible, actively engaged manager of your own healthcare experience.

Creating a Responsibility Mindset about Your Healthcare

Seeing healthcare as a personal responsibility will undoubtedly take some time to permeate our culture, but it is imperative from a systems science perspective that we all develop this mindset. If the overall objective of the US healthcare system is to optimize benefits (how healthcare is organized and paid for) and care (the delivery of high-quality results) across our entire population, then we need to put that into context for individuals and families. So, given your life stage, your health status, your economic situation, and your personal values, how do you think about optimizing the benefits and care available to you and your family—that is, getting the best value for each healthcare dollar you spend? As Americans, we need to think systematically in both the short and long term, taking into account not only what choices are most convenient for us at the moment but also the implications our decisions and actions may have in terms of cost, quality, and efficiency across the system. Hoping that other people are going to solve the healthcare crisis for us, either at a national or individual level, is not a plan. Like Sarah and her family in chapter 8, we have to get much more actively involved.

In virtually all major areas of our lives—except in healthcare—we have a fairly solid understanding of how our actions have an impact on our life goals. For example, although we are entitled to public education through twelfth grade, we realize that how we perform during that time, coupled with the choices we make about whether and where to continue our education after high school, can have a significant impact on the quality of our lives. Most of us know that without higher education, there are certain jobs, professions, and opportunities that simply won't be available to us. As a person who has been genetically disadvantaged with a major illness, I recognize that people are born with and grow up with many relative advantages and disadvantages that can alter the personal landscape of their lives, including the pursuit of higher education. And in using education as an example, I am sensitive to how disadvantaging factors contribute to the dismal statistics regarding high school graduation rates in our country. But I think the vast majority of people in our country would agree that, in spite of these challenges, a systematic objective of our educational system should be to educate students so they graduate from high school with at least a minimum set of competencies.

Similarly, in the realm of personal finances, we make the connection between our actions and our life goals by deliberately trying to save money and arranging financing for major events such as college, weddings, home ownership, vacations, and retirement. In fact, one of the first pieces of systematic advice we receive as young adults entering the workforce is to begin thinking about retirement savings by contributing as much money as possible to retirement plans in a manner that maximizes our tax-deferred savings and takes advantage of any matching arrangement our employer may offer. In other words, we take disciplined action today to help create the possibility of a better and more predictable financial future. We seem to understand that if we don't save a sufficient amount of money during our working lives, we may not be able to retire as well, travel as much, or live where we prefer to live. But we don't yet think this way in terms of healthcare.

One of These Things Is Not Like the Others

When I was a kid, I watched the television show *Sesame Street*, which had a repeating musical segment entitled "One of These Things Is Not Like the Others." They showed four items, one of which just didn't fit in with the other items. Perhaps that musical game was what drove my initial interest in systems science. Little did I know then how perfectly it would sum up our nation's view of healthcare insurance relative to other important parts of our lives. So let's see how this game would play out regarding important decisions we make as adults today. When we buy homes, we make monthly mortgage payments, and we *also* buy homeowners insurance to protect our investment. When we buy cars, we make monthly car payments and *also* buy automobile insurance in the event that we have an accident. However, the way we regard our healthcare is simply not like these other examples. When we obtain health insurance, we make monthly premium payments for our healthcare coverage, but we do *not* also buy separate insurance in case something goes seriously wrong. The healthcare system most of us are familiar with is a hybrid type of insurance coverage that is expected to do the following: give us access to doctors and hospitals, provide prenegotiated discounts when we do pay out of pocket (a benefit of health coverage that most people do not even think about), pay the lion's share of the normal cost of our healthcare beyond deductibles and co-payments, and provide catastrophic protection against exceptionally expensive healthcare costs. It is important to realize that we expect much more from healthcare insurance than we do from all the other kinds of insurance we buy. Healthcare insurance definitely is not like the others!

Despite the fact that healthcare accounts for more than 17 percent of the US gross domestic product,[4] most working people do not consciously budget or save for the healthcare expenses they will inevitably incur out of pocket while employed, or later when they may no longer have health insurance through their employer. They also appear not to make a direct connection between investing in their health now and having the quality of life they want later (including the ability to pursue other goals). As a nation, we have a substantially longer life expectancy than in decades past, and if we're fortunate to live to age sixty-five or beyond, then it is almost certain that healthcare will be one of the more expensive and time-consuming aspects of our lives. If Ben Franklin were alive today, he might be tempted to modify his famous quote to say, "In this world nothing can be said to be certain but death, taxes and *healthcare expenses*." Given what we know about our increasing need for care as we get older, it is systematically illogical not to add healthcare to the long list of items we need to pay for each month, and for which we need to save.

Medicare May Not Be Our Safety Net

While I want to steer clear of social policy in this book, a systems approach does require the consideration of social systems. Why don't most people save or plan for their healthcare expenses? For most of us, I believe there are two reasons. First, we generally know little about how the healthcare system operates, and we have not been educated to think of healthcare as a financial planning category. Second, most of us assume that when we reach a certain age, the Medicare program will provide our health coverage. But it doesn't really matter whether we believe that health coverage in our senior years is an inalienable right or not; from a systems perspective, it is what it is—uncertain. And just as people were shocked when the financial meltdown in 2008 altered their long-standing assumptions about their retirement plans and home values, people need to consider that the government may have a significantly diminished capacity to provide healthcare benefits to our older citizens compared to what it has now. This is due in part to the fact that the Medicare system was not designed with the expectation that life expectancy would increase so significantly.

While most of us have heard that the Social Security program may run out of money, few of us know that the Medicare Part A Trust is projected to go bankrupt within the next decade if things don't change.[5] And currently, although the US government does make a distinction between your retirement contributions to the Social Security system and your healthcare contributions to Medicare, the numbers are not proportionately correct, given the cost of healthcare compared to other retirement expenses. Currently, we pay a 1.45 percent tax rate for Medicare and a 6.2 percent tax rate for Social Security.[6] From a systems perspective (regardless of whether you think there should be a single-payer, government-run healthcare system or whether private insurers should continue to play a role), either the Medicare taxes will need to substantially increase, or the respective amounts of the Medicare and Social Security taxes will need to be allocated differently if we are to prevent Medicare from going bankrupt. Regardless of your perspective on social program taxation, we must get more healthcare for each dollar spent by applying Integrated Healthcare Management principles with rigor to the senior population and with extra tenacity for those seniors with multiple chronic health conditions. Doing so is both humane and fiscally responsible.

Societal Responsibility: Systematic Education Early and Often

I have talked throughout this book about consumers becoming actively engaged in their own healthcare. Molly Mettler, a friend of mine who, along with her husband, Don Kemper, created a highly successful consumer healthcare content company, aptly summed up this healthcare imperative by saying, "Consumers are the greatest untapped resource in healthcare. If we want to build a better healthcare system, we must first build a better patient." I believe that this is an important and accurate statement. IHM will go a long way toward making us all better consumers by using systematic principles and information technology to drive the right information to the right person in the right place at the right time. However, we need to start preparing people much sooner and much more thoroughly to successfully navigate the healthcare jungle.

When I took my high school's required health class, we learned a bit about anatomy; we were taught that certain parts of our anatomy were useful for reproduction; we were lectured on how to avoid sexually transmitted diseases; and we viewed countless video clips about how illegal drugs will turn our brains into eggs in a frying pan. We also learned a little about both nutrition and personal hygiene. In speaking with high school students today, not much has changed, except that now they can choose to take the class online, thereby avoiding the embarrassment of discussing these topics with classmates of varying maturity levels.

What if we were to modify the curriculum not just to teach the anatomical systems of the body, but also to tell students about different types of healthcare providers, about what specialists correspond with which particular human body systems, about common diseases such as diabetes and heart disease, and about the positive steps we can take in support of our own longer-term health? What if we were to introduce students to the major elements of the healthcare supply chain so they could better understand primary and preventive care; specialty care; and the general purpose of hospitals, diagnostic centers, and pharmacies—giving these young people a chance to become intelligent healthcare consumers? And what if we were to teach them to budget healthcare into their lives as an assumed monthly expense (like food, clothing, rent, and transportation) and educate them enough about the types of healthcare coverage so they would be more likely to give it some serious thought as they enter the work force? When these former students enter the work force, what if we were to teach them to save for healthcare in the way we save for retirement? Basic education about healthcare funding mechanisms might actually encourage people to plan for their future healthcare expenses. If the government recognizes that there are two separate "buckets" to which people need to contribute money for their future—healthcare and retirement—then so should every consumer. But many consumers do not have the knowledge to come to this conclusion on their own. Comprehensive education starting when people are young and continuing into their early adulthood makes systematic sense if we expect consumers to understand and actively engage in important decisions about their health and healthcare expenses over a lifetime.

Personal Responsibility: Your Behavior Affects Your Bottom Line

By now you must have a sense of how I would answer the opening questions of this chapter. Healthcare is most definitely a responsibility. But it is also an opportunity. If you take the view that as you get older there is a good chance you will need more medical care, then expecting your government to take care of all your healthcare needs for the rest of your life is essentially playing a high-risk game. Proactively planning for your future healthcare needs is the only way to ensure that you will be able to pay for your healthcare in your later years. Similarly, it is incumbent upon all of us to look at our behaviors as they relate to our health. We must accept the fact that if we fail to stop smoking, if we do not keep our weight down or commit to regular exercise, or if we choose other behaviors shown by evidence-based medicine to adversely affect our health, then we may need more care, and from a systems science perspective, it is logical that we might be expected to pay more for our healthcare.

As we have seen in previous chapters of this book, when it comes to understanding the cost of healthcare, we each need to take on a more retail-oriented mindset. In other words, by learning how much different components of healthcare actually cost and creating a culture of health where each of us is conscious of the value we receive for each healthcare dollar spent, we will all help drive greater efficiency in healthcare, just as we have in other industries. Moreover, by taking responsibility for our day-to-day behaviors and healthcare spending, along with financial planning for future healthcare needs, we have the opportunity to influence whether we achieve our lifelong goals.

On the Healthcare Horizon

Of course, as I know far too well, there are many people who are genetically disadvantaged and, through no fault of their own, will require more care at greater cost than others. The healthcare system must be designed to allow for these types of cases, in which the medical needs of individuals cannot be controlled or determined by their behaviors, and to ensure that these people are not excluded from organized systems of benefits and care. The Accountable Care Act legislation creates a mechanism to move us in this direction. While it is true that taking care of people with significant chronic illness is relatively expensive, it will be even more expensive in total if we wait for catastrophic things to occur, which is often the case when people are excluded from coverage for preexisting conditions. The good news, however, is that because the medical research component of our healthcare system is so sophisticated, over time, people who have been "genetically picked on" will have more weapons with which to fight back. And by using IHM principles to help identify and segment consumers into groupings that can systematically give them the best information and evidence-based care available, we can deliver a high-quality healthcare experience to more people.

On the Brink of Unmitigated Success

I will leave it to the philosophers and policy makers to calculate the cost of a human life and to determine how much should be spent to save it. But I will say that if we apply IHM principles to the US healthcare system, our overall health status will improve, we will spend less and receive better care for each dollar spent, and we will free up more money for policy makers to determine how to spend or save.

As IHM enters the marketplace as a basis for reforming our healthcare system in a sustainable and affordable way, you should expect and demand the following:

- Greater transparency on the actual price of healthcare services, drugs, and supplies
- Benefits that are tailored or personalized for you and members of your family
- A regularly updated health improvement plan and aligned incentives among you and your physicians to support your health goals
- A personal health record containing demographic, health history, and benefits data (filled in and updated automatically by your health plan) that you can take with you if you change health plans, and to which you control access by providers and family members
- Physician office and hospital clinical systems that use electronic medical records and electronic health records to improve quality of care, efficiency, and patient safety
- A more cooperative and less adversarial relationship between your health plan and your providers, who will work together on your behalf
- Better access to information about evidence-based medicine guidelines (for both consumers and doctors) so that you and your doctor can make informed decisions about your care
- Systematic education starting in public (and private) schools regarding health behaviors, how the healthcare system is organized, and how to budget and save for healthcare expenses
- Personal responsibility on your part for making informed decisions with your doctor about your healthcare treatment options, improving everyday behaviors (such as following the current guidelines for daily exercise and nutrition), and managing your current and longer-term healthcare financial planning
- Opportunities for you to participate in secure online social networking communities with other consumers who have a similar

health status, life stage, economic status, and personal values, and to have these interactions supported by reliable, evidence-based educational information

- Ability to use technology for timely communication with your providers through secure e-mail and online e-visits as a way to speed up access and save time

Now that you have read this book, the list above may appear to be common sense. Likewise, your expectations of what our healthcare system can become may be higher. I hope that both statements are true. As a knowledgeable healthcare consumer, you are empowered to undertake your personal responsibilities while also keeping pressure on the various constituents in the system to perform in a manner that increases healthcare value for each of us individually and for our society as a whole. Playing the blame game, as we sometimes witness in the headlines, never successfully resolves deficiencies in a system. But by becoming informed and actively engaged, you can help our healthcare system come closer to realizing its potential, as well as your expectations.

Conclusion:
Let's Get Moving

W e are at a critical juncture for healthcare in the United States. By following the systematic principles of Integrated Healthcare Management (IHM), we will be able to solve our affordability and quality crisis in a sustainable way. IHM is an information-sharing framework that recognizes that health benefits and the spectrum of care must be coordinated among constituents. IHM addresses the root causes that perpetuate today's misaligned incentives and looks at healthcare as a whole system. And IHM does so in a way that can build upon today's public and private systems while enabling healthcare reform efforts. Realistically, we could not realign a two-trillion-dollar-plus industry without connecting current realities to IHM's future framework. Every system must be designed and structured to achieve a particular goal—and no matter our social policy with regard to levels of funding, we must pursue the goal of creating the greatest healthcare value for each healthcare dollar we spend. Like other industries, we must adopt a mindset that the value we expect for each healthcare dollar spent will continuously increase over time and that the cost of care will not automatically increase each year. In this way, we will be able to free up capacity to include the uninsured and underinsured in an organized system of benefits and care.

We built the definition of IHM with the consumer as the focal point and with the acknowledgment that the consumer is on the demand side of a complex supply chain. At TriZetto, we define IHM as *the systematic application of processes and shared information to optimize the coordination of benefits and care for the healthcare consumer.* You now know, from reading this book, that consumers, providers, employers, brokers, and payers (both public and private) are all constituent components of this system. You also have a better understanding of how different supply-chain processes, applied technologies, information technologies, constituent behaviors, and incentives work today and will need to work differently as we move toward IHM. Throughout the book, you have seen that IHM requires health plans and providers to attain a higher level of cooperation and providers and consumers to achieve a higher level of coordination. And you have seen that a variety of rich information sources exist that, when converged, will lead to tailored benefits and care for individuals. Chapter 10 is meant to emphasize that even if all the other constituents do their part, we as healthcare consumers must be actively engaged. It is the duty of our society to educate consumers early and often about the important role healthcare and its associated expense play throughout our lives. And as consumers, it is up to us to actively participate in our healthcare decision making and to plan for the day-to-day expenses and future costs we hope to live long enough to incur.

Just imagine the best of benefits administration and the best of care management converging at the right place, at the right time, to optimize your own healthcare while also improving our nation's healthcare system as a whole. IHM places this future imminently within our grasp.

Acknowledgments

In my experience, few people read acknowledgments. I hope these are read.

After a reasonably healthy childhood, I was "blessed" with a challenging and painful illness, Crohn's disease, in the midst of my college education. I carried this blessing into my marriage, through my early working years, and into fatherhood. Somehow, I arrived as a young adult in a time when digital computing and communications technology, accounting, cost management, process management, information management, and reengineered industry models explosively converged. In my early career at Andersen Consulting (now Accenture), I was invested in, and given a chance to explore multiple industries such as banking, mining, and manufacturing, as well as multiple functions such as accounting, finance, operations, marketing, and sales. As I began to specialize as a consultant in the healthcare industry, I met a group of people, many of whom I am still privileged to work with today.

Still very ill and in daily physical pain and discomfort, I became entrenched in the healthcare industry at the advent of managed care. I lived it firsthand, as I helped run it at Comprecare, TakeCare, and FHP International. I was handed the reins of information technology in increasingly large organizations by CEOs who had the courage to support a very young executive. And I was surrounded by inventors, trying to figure out how to create affordable, accessible, and high-quality healthcare in a manner that wouldn't break the bank of employers and consumers. We tried many ideas, and many of them worked, while some of them failed. I learned that failure was most often a result of highly capable people pitting themselves against one another as equal and opposing forces. And I learned that my role, even though I was regarded as the "systems" guy, was to converge ideas that seemed irreconcilable. You gain the perspective to do this if at eight a.m. you are debating a group of physicians about data quality, at ten you are reviewing an electronic medical record implementation, at two p.m. you are designing ways to properly reimburse primary care physicians for the increased value they bring, and at eleven you literally are having your life saved by a surgeon and gastroenterologist working together on your behalf while the anesthesiologist (knowing your background) inquires about aspects of managed care reimbursement as he is putting you under.

And so my first acknowledgment is to all the people I have encountered who are good at what they do, are set in their ways, and do not easily change their perspectives. You each inspire me to create fusion—so much more powerful than divisive behavior—when fission is the status quo.

Then, of course, there is this book, *The Healthcare Cure*. It is an inadequate but encompassing synthesis that is intended to help people take a step back from a very complex challenge and then step back in to attack it again. While I have tried to articulate principles that have been vetted over twenty-five years, I intend to keep learning by listening to the viewpoints of all constituents. The book would never have resulted in a fully written form without the collaboration of Karin Leinwand, who patiently and persistently made sure that the words on the page expressed their intended meaning. Hugh Kennedy kept us on point and reminded us that we needed to turn the ideas into a consumable deliverable. Laura Fitzgerald, as she has been for years, was my metronome. Linda Bernier's rare intellect and good humor kept us sane. Mark Cranston kept us on schedule while ensuring that content was not compromised. Contributors, reviewers and fact checkers included David Algeo, Larry Bridge, Debi Curbey, Stephen Furia, Eric Grossman, Ryan Larson, Marty Mattei, Dave Pinkert, Brad Samson, Jim Sullivan, Tom Main, Mike Watkins, and my longtime business associate and friend—and an IHM progenitor in his own right—Dan Spirek.

My wife, daughters, and extended family make all efforts to improve the world worthwhile.

To Integrated Healthcare Management!

—*Jeff*

Notes

Foreword

1. US Census Bureau, *Statistical Abstract of the United States: 2011* (Washington, DC: Bureau of Census, 2011), p. 109.

Chapter 1: Taking a Systems Approach

1. Department of Health and Human Services, "Office of the National Coordinator for Health Information Technology: Health Information Technology," http://www.hhs.gov/recovery/reports/plans/onc_hit.pdf (accessed March 11, 2011).

Chapter 2: The Blind Men and the Elephant: Lessons for Healthcare

1. American Medical Association, "About AMA," http://www.ama-assn.org/ama/pub/about-ama/physician-data-resources.shtml (accessed March 8, 2011).
2. American Hospital Association, "Fast Facts on US Hospitals," http://www.aha.org/aha/resource-center/Statistics-and-Studies/fast-facts.html (accessed March 8, 2011).
3. Ibid.
4. Kaiser Family Foundation, "United States: Prescription Drugs," StateHealthFacts.org, http://www.statehealthfacts.org/profileind.jsp?sub=66&rgn=1&cat=5 (accessed March 8, 2011).
5. TriZetto internal research.

6. Ibid.

7. Christopher J. Truffer et al., "Health Spending Projections through 2019: The Recession's Impact Continues," *Health Affairs* 29, no. 3 (March 2010): 522–29.

Chapter 3: The Lexus and the Human

1. Therese A. Stukel, F. Lee Lucas, and David E. Wennberg, "Long-Term Outcomes of Regional Variations in Intensity of Invasive vs. Medical Management of Medicare Patients with Acute Myocardial Infarction," *JAMA* 293, no. 11 (March 16, 2005): 1329–37.

2. Dartmouth Institute for Health Policy and Clinical Practice, "Q&A with Dr. Jack Wennberg: What's Wrong with the US Health-Care System?" Dartmouth Atlas of Health Care, http://www.dartmouthatlas.org/downloads/press/Wennberg_interviews_DartMed.pdf (accessed March 11, 2009).

3. Atul Gawande, *The Checklist Manifesto: How to Get Things Right* (New York: Picador, 2010), pp. 12–13.

Chapter 4: Understanding the Healthcare Supply Chain

1. TriZetto internal research; John Holahan, "The 2007–09 Recession and Health Insurance Coverage," *Health Affairs* 30, no. 1 (January 2011): 145–52.

2. TriZetto internal research.

3. TriZetto internal analysis of multiple data sources, including 2006 Insurance Department Resources Report, National Association of Insurance Commissioners; National Association of Health Underwriters; Independent Insurance Agents and Brokers of America.

4. US Census Bureau, "US and World Population Clocks," http://www.census.gov/main/www/popclock.html (accessed March 8, 2011).

5. Michael E. Martinez and Robin A. Cohen, "Health Insurance Coverage: Early Release of Estimates from the National Health Interview Survey, January–September 2009," Division of Health Interview Statistics, National Center for Health Statistics, (March 2010), http://www.cdc.gov/nchs/data/nhis/earlyrelease/insur201003.pdf (accessed March 11, 2011).

6. US Census Bureau, *Statistical Abstract of the United States: 2011* (Washington, DC: Bureau of Census, 2011), p. 109.

7. TriZetto internal research.

8. Centers for Medicare and Medicaid Services, "Medicare Enrollment: National Trends," https://www.cms.gov/MedicareEnRpts/Downloads/HISMI 2009.pdf (accessed March 8, 2011).

9. Kaiser Family Foundation, "Medicaid Enrollment: December 2009 Data Snapshot," http://www.kff.org/medicaid/upload/8050-02.pdf (accessed March 8, 2011).

10. TRICARE, "What Is TRICARE?," http://tricare.mil/mybenefit/ ProfileFilter.do?puri=/home/overview/WhatIsTRICARE (accessed March 9, 2011).

11. Congressional Budget Office, "Potential Costs of Veterans' Health Care," http://www.cbo.gov/ftpdocs/118xx/doc11811/2010_10_7_VAHealthcare _Summary.pdf (accessed March 9, 2011).

12. US Office of Personnel Management, "The Federal Employees Health Benefits Program (FEHB)," Indian Health Service, http://www.ihs.gov/Public Affairs/DirCorner/docs/FEHB_BASICS.pdf (accessed March 9, 2011).

13. Merritt Hawkins, "2010 Review of Physician Recruiting Incentives," http://www.merritthawkins.com/uploadedFiles/MerrittHawkings/Surveys/ mha2010incentivesurvPDF.pdf (accessed March 10, 2011).

14. John E. Wennberg et al., "An Agenda for Change: Improving Quality and Curbing Health Care Spending: Opportunities for the Congress and the Obama Administration," Dartmouth Institute for Health Policy and Clinical Practice, *Dartmouth Atlas of Health Care*, December 2008, http://www.dartmouthatlas .org/downloads/reports/agenda_for_change.pdf (accessed July 16, 2011).

Chapter 5: The Perspectives of Healthcare Constituents

1. John Holahan, "The 2007–09 Recession and Health Insurance Coverage," *Health Affairs* 30, no. 1 (January 2011): 145–52.

2. World Self-Medication Industry, "Responsible Self-Care and Self-Medication: A Worldwide Review of Consumer Surveys," http://www.wsmi.org/ pdf/wsmibro3.pdf (accessed July 22, 2011).

3. American Medical Association, "Bolster Primary Care: Avert a Physician

Shortage," http://www.ama-assn.org/amednews/2009/01/05/edsa0105.htm (accessed March 8, 2011).

4. Ibid.

5. TriZetto internal analysis of multiple data sources, including 2006 Insurance Department Resources Report, National Association of Insurance Commissioners; National Association of Health Underwriters; Independent Insurance Agents and Brokers of America.

Chapter 6: Information Silos: A Fragmented System

1. American Diabetes Association, "Choose to Live: Your Diabetes Survival Guide," http://www.diabetes.org/assets/pdfs/winning-at-work/chooseguide.pdf (accessed March 11, 2011).

2. Joslin Diabetes Center, "Guidelines for Preserving Vision," http://www.joslin.org/care/guidelines_for_preserving_vision.html (accessed March 11, 2011).

3. Center for the Evaluative Clinical Services, "Effective Care," *Dartmouth Atlas of Health Care*, http://www.dartmouthatlas.org/downloads/reports/effective_care.pdf (accessed March 11, 2011).

4. Ibid.

5. Dartmouth Institute for Health Policy and Clinical Practice, "Supply-Sensitive Care," *Dartmouth Atlas of Health Care*, http://www.dartmouthatlas.org/keyissues/issue.aspx?con=2937 (accessed March 11, 2011).

Chapter 7: Follow the Dollar

1. Christopher J. Truffer et al., "Health Spending Projections through 2019: The Recession's Impact Continues," *Health Affairs* 29, no. 3 (March 2010): 522–29.

2. TriZetto internal analysis of healthcare industry sources, including Medicare and Medicaid data and commercial data.

Chapter 8: Integrated Healthcare Management: The Solution

1. Zareth N. Irwin et al., "Variation in Surgical Decision Making for Degenerative Spinal Disorders. Part I: Lumbar Spine," *Spine* 30, no. 19 (October 1, 2005): 2208–13, http://www.medscape.com/viewarticle/515413 (accessed March 10, 2011).

2. John E. Wennberg et al., "An Agenda for Change: Improving Quality and Curbing Health Care Spending: Opportunities for the Congress and the Obama Administration," Dartmouth Institute for Health Policy and Clinical Practice, *Dartmouth Atlas of Health Care*, December 2008, http://www.dartmouthatlas .org/downloads/reports/agenda_for_change.pdf (accessed July 16, 2011).

3. Thomas J. Main (untitled presentation to TriZetto Group, Newport Beach, CA, November 2008).

4. Ibid.

Chapter 9: Digital Alphabet Soup: Understanding EHRs, EMRs and PHRs

1. Chun-Ju Hsia et al., "Electronic Medical Record/Electronic Health Record Systems of Office-Based Physicians: United States, 2009 and Preliminary 2010 State Estimates," Centers for Disease Control and Prevention, http:// www.cdc.gov/nchs/data/hestat/emr_ehr_09/emr_ehr_09.pdf (accessed March 8, 2011).

2. Ibid.

3. TriZetto internal analysis of healthcare industry sources, including Medicare and Medicaid data and commercial data.

4. Brian Montopoli, "Obama: Health Care Reform Is a Moral—and Fiscal—Imperative," *CBS News*, March 5, 2009, http://www.cbsnews.com/8301 -503544_162-4845451-503544.html (accessed March 8, 2011).

Chapter 10: Personal Responsibility and Societal Opportunity

1. Frances M. Chevarley, "Total Medication and Prescription Expenditures by Current Asthma Status and Whether Asthma Daily Preventive Medicine Is Being Taken, United States, 2006," Agency for Healthcare Research and Quality,

http://meps.ahrq.gov/mepsweb/data_files/publications/st241/stat241.shtml (accessed March 10, 2011).

2. Agency for Healthcare Research and Quality, "Emergency Room Services: Mean and Median Expenses per Person with Expense and Distribution of Expenses by Source of Payment: United States, 2008. Medical Expenditure Panel Survey Household Component Data," http://www.meps.ahrq.gov/mepsweb/ data_stats/MEPS_topics.jsp?topicid=5Z-1 (accessed March 10, 2011).

3. Kimberley Strassel, "Mr. Burd Goes to Washington: Business Will Pay for Government Health Care," *Wall Street Journal*, June 19, 2009, http://online.wsj .com/article/SB124536722522229323.html (accessed July 15, 2011).

4. Christopher J. Truffer et al., "Health Spending Projections through 2019: The Recession's Impact Continues," *Health Affairs* 29, no. 3 (March 2010): 522–29.

5. Centers for Medicare and Medicaid Services, "CMS Roadmaps Overview," http://www.cms.gov/QualityInitiativesGenInfo/downloads/Roadmap Overview_OEA_1-16.pdf (accessed March 8, 2011).

6. Social Security Administration, "Social Security and Medicare Tax Rates," http://www.ssa.gov/OACT/ProgData/taxRates.html (accessed March 8, 2011).

Index